Ultimate Crockpot Recipes

Table Of Contents

All Day Crockpot Delight

2-3 lbs. boneless chuck, cut into 1 inch cubes
1/2 c. flour
1/4 c. butter
1 onion, sliced
1 tsp. salt
1/8 tsp. pepper
1 clove garlic, minced
2 c. beer
1/4 c. flour

Coat beef cubes with the 1/2 cup flour. Brown melted butter. Drain off excess fat. In crock pot, combine browned meat with onion, salt, pepper, garlic and beer. Cover and cook on low 5-7 hours until meat is tender. Turn control to high. Dissolve remaining 1/4 cup flour in small amount of water. Stir into meat mixture, cook on high 30-40 minutes. Serve with rice and salad.

All Day Macaroni And Cheese

8 ounces elbow macaroni, cooked and drained
4 cups (16 ounces) shredded sharp cheddar cheese
1 cans (12 ounces) evaporated milk
1 1/2 cups milk
2 eggs
1 teaspoon salt
1/2 teaspoon black pepper

Place the cooked macaroni in crock pot that has been sprayed with nonstick cooking spray. Add the remaining ingredients, all except 1 cup of the cheese, mix well. sprinkle with the remaining 1 cup of cheese and then cover and cook on low setting for 5 to 6 hours or until the mixture is firm and golden around the edges. Do not remove the cover or stir until it has finished cooking.

Apple Brown Betty

3 lbs. cooking apples
10 slices of bread, cubed (about 4 cups)
1/2 tsp. cinnamon
1/4 tsp. nutmeg
1/8 tsp. salt

3/4 c. brown sugar
1/2 c. butter or margarine, melted

Wash apples, peel, core, cut into eighths; place in bottom on crock. Combine bread cubes, cinnamon, nutmeg, salt, sugar, butter; toss together. Place on top of apples in crock. Cover. Place crock into outer shell. Cook on low setting 2 to 4 hours. Makes 6 to 8 servings.

Apple Butter

4 qts. Unsweetened applesauce
7 c. granulated sugar
1-1/3 c. brown sugar
5-1/3 t. cider vinegar
5-1/3 t. lemon juice
2 teaspoon cinnamon
2 teaspoon allspice
1 teaspoon ground cloves

Combine all ingredients in a crock pot or roasting pan. Cover and cook 3 hours, stirring occasionally. remove lid and continue cooking until excess liquid cooks away (turn to low as necessary) crock pot 5-8 hours, oven 3-5 hours seal mixture in hot jars and process in a hot water bath for 10 minutes. Makes approximately 8-10 pints.

Apple Coconut Crisp

4 large granny smith apples, peeled & coarsely sliced (about 4 cups)
1/2 cup sweetened flaked coconut
1 tablespoon flour
1/3 cup brown sugar
1/2 cup butterscotch or caramel ice cream topping
1/2 teaspoon cinnamon
1/3 cup flour
1/2 cup quick rolled oats
2 tablespoons butter or margarine

In a casserole 1 1/2-quart baking dish that fits in the crock pot, combine apples with coconut, 1 tablespoon flour, 1/3 cup brown sugar, and cinnamon. Drizzle with the ice cream topping. Combine remaining ingredients in a small bowl with a fork or pastry cutter and sprinkle over apple mixture. Cover and cook on high for 2 1/2 to 3 hours, until apples are tender. Serve warm with vanilla ice cream or whipped topping.

Apple Cranberry Compote

6 cooking apples, peeled, slice
1 cup fresh cranberries
1 cup sugar
1/2 teaspoons grated orange peel
1/2 cups water
1/4 cups port wine
Sour cream

Arrange apple slices and cranberries in crock pot. Sprinkle sugar over fruit. Add orange peel, water and wine. Stir to mix ingredients. Cover, cook on low 4-6 hours, until apples are tender. Serve warm fruits with the juices, topped with a dab of sour cream. Serves 6.

Apple Cranberry Crisp

3 apples
1 cup cranberries
3/4 cup brown sugar
1/3 cup rolled oats
1/4 tsp. salt
1 tsp. cinnamon
1/3 cup butter, softened

Peel, core and slice apples. Place apple slices and cranberries in crock pot. Mix remaining ingredients in separate bowl and sprinkle over top of apple and cranberries. Place 4 or 5 paper towels over the top of the crock pot place an object across the top of the crock pot and set lid on top. This allows the steam to escape. Turn crock pot on high and cook for about 2 hours. Serves 4.

Apple Date Pudding

4-5 apples, peeled, cored and diced
3/4 cup sugar, or less, to taste
1/2 cup chopped dates
1/2 cup toasted, chopped pecans
2 tbs. flour
1 tsp. baking powder

1/8 tsp. salt
1/4 tsp. nutmeg
2 tbs. melted butter
1 egg, beaten

In the crock pot, place apples, sugar, dates and pecans; stir. In a separate bowl, mix together flour, baking powder, salt and nutmeg and stir into apple mixture. Drizzle melted butter over batter and stir. Stir in egg. Set cooker on low and cook for 3 to 4 hours. Serve warm.

Apple Glazed Pork Roast

4 lb. pork loin roast
6 apples
1/4 cup apple juice
3 t. brown sugar
1 t. ginger, ground

Rub roast with salt and pepper. Brown pork roasts under broiler to remove excess fat; drain well. Core and quarter apples. Place apple quarters in bottom of crock pot. Place roast on top of apples. Combine apple juice, brown sugar, and ginger. Spoon over top surface of roast, moistening well. Cover and cook on low for 10-12 hours, until done.

Apple Nut Cheesecake

Crust:
1 cup graham cracker crumbs
1/2 teaspoon cinnamon
2 tablespoons sugar
3 tablespoons butter, melted
1/4 cup finely chopped pecans or walnuts

Filling:
16 ounces cream cheese
1/4 cup brown sugar
1/2 cup granulated white sugar
2 large eggs
3 tablespoons heavy whipping cream
1 tablespoon cornstarch
1 teaspoon vanilla

Topping:
1 large apple, thinly sliced (about 1 1/2 cups)
1 teaspoon cinnamon
1/4 cup sugar
1 tablespoon finely chopped pecans or walnuts

Combine crust ingredients; pat into a 7-inch spring form pan. Beat sugars into cream cheese until smooth and creamy. Beat in eggs, whipping cream, cornstarch, and vanilla. Beat for about 3 minutes on medium speed of a hand-held electric mixer. Pour mixture into the prepared crust. Combine apple slices with sugar, cinnamon and nuts; place topping evenly over the top of cheesecake. Place the cheesecake on a rack (or "ring" of aluminum foil to keep it off the bottom of the pot) in the crock pot. Cover and cook on high for 2 1/2 to 3 hours. Let stand in the covered pot (after turning it off) for about 1 to 2 hours, until cool enough to handle. Cool thoroughly before removing pan sides. Chill before serving; store leftovers in the refrigerator.

Apple Pie Coffee Cake

Apple mixture:
1 can (20 oz) apple pie filling, apple slices broken up somewhat
1/2 teaspoon cinnamon
3 tablespoons brown sugar

Cake batter:
2 small yellow cake mixes
2 eggs, beaten
1/2 cup sour cream
3 tablespoons softened butter or margarine
1/2 cup evaporated milk
1/2 teaspoon cinnamon
1 teaspoon butter or margarine for greasing crock pot

Combine ingredients for apple mixture in a small bowl. Combine batter ingredients; mix well. Generously butter the sides and bottom of a 3 1/2 quart crock pot. Spread about half the apple mixture in the bottom of the pot. Spoon 1/2 the batter over the apple mixture. Spoon the remaining apple mixture over the batter, and then cover with remaining batter. Cover and cook on high for 2 to 2 1/2 hours. Turn heat off, leave cover ajar slightly, and cool for about 15 minutes. Invert on a plate, retrieving any apples left in the bottom of the pot and placing on top of the cake.

Apple Pudding Cake

2 cups sugar
1 cup vegetable oil
2 eggs
2 teaspoons vanilla
2 cups flour
1 teaspoon baking soda
1 teaspoon nutmeg
2 cups unpeeled apple, finely chopped
1 cup chopped nuts (walnuts or pecans)

Beat sugar, oil, eggs, and vanilla. Add apple with dry ingredients and mix well. Spray a two pound tin can with cooking spray or grease and flour it well. Pour batter into can, filling no more than 2/3 full. Place can in crock pot. Do not add water. Cover but leave cover ajar so steam can escape. Cook on high 3 1/2 to 4 hours. Don't peek before the last hour of baking. Cake is done when top is set. Let stand in can a few minutes before tipping pudding out on a plate.

Applesauce Sauerkraut

4 cups sauerkraut, rinsed and drained
2 cups sweetened applesauce
1/2 tsp caraway seeds
1 tbs butter or margarine

Combine all ingredients. Place in a greased 2 quart casserole. Bake at 375° f. for 30 to 45 minutes. Serves 6.

Apricot Nut Bread

3/4 cup dried apricots
1 cup flour
2 tsp baking powder
1/4 tsp baking soda
1/2 tsp salt
1/2 cup sugar
3/4 cup milk
1 egg, slightly beaten
1 tbsp grated orange peel
1 tbsp vegetable oil
1/2 cup whole wheat flour
1 cup coarsely chopped walnuts

Place the apricots on a chopping block. Sprinkle 1 t flour over them. Dip a knife into the flour and chop the apricots finely. Flour the knife often to keep the cutup fruit from sticking together. Sift the remaining flour, baking powder, baking soda, salt and sugar into a large bowl. Combine the milk, egg, orange peel, and oil. Stir the flour mixture and the whole wheat flour. Fold in the cut up apricots, any flour left on the cutting block and the walnuts. Pour into a well greased, floured baking unit. Cover and place on a rack in the crock pot, but prop the lid open a fraction with a toothpick or a twist of foil to let excess steam escape. Cook on high for 4 to 6 hours. Cool on a rack for 10 minutes. Serve warm or cold. Makes 4 to 6 servings.

Artichoke & Cheese Dip

1 lb. shredded mozzarella
1 c. grated parmesan
1 c. (8 oz. jar) mayonnaise
1 c. (8 1/2 oz.) artichoke hearts, drained and chopped
Minced onions

Mix ingredients together. Bake in casserole at 350 degrees for 20-30 minutes or in lightly buttered 3 1/2 quart crock pot on (high) for about 1 hour. Serve with broken up French bread or wheat crackers.

Asparagus Casserole

2 cans sliced asparagus, (10 oz each)
1 can cream of celery soup, (10 oz)
2 hard cooked eggs, thinly sliced
1 cup grated cheddar cheese
1/2 cup coarsely crushed saltines or Ritz crackers
1 teaspoon butter

Place drained asparagus in lightly buttered crock pot or crock pot baking insert. Combine soup and cheese. Top asparagus with sliced eggs, soup mixture, and then the cracker crumbs. Dot with butter. Cover and cook on low for 4 to 6 hours.

Bacon Cheese Dip

16 slices bacon, diced, fried and drained
2 8-ounce packages cream cheese, softened and cubed
4 cups shredded cheddar cheese
1 cup half-and-half
2 teaspoons Worcestershire sauce

1 teaspoon dried minced onion
1/2 teaspoon dry mustard
1/2 teaspoon salt
Dash hot sauce

Put all ingredients in the crock pot and cook on low, stirring occasionally until cheese melts, about 1 hour. Taste and adjust seasonings, add bacon, and keep on low to serve. Serve with cubed or sliced French bread.

Baked Apples

6 lg. cooking apples
3/4 c. orange juice
2 tsp. grated orange rind
1 tsp. lemon rind grated
3/4 c. rose wine
1/4 tsp. cinnamon
1/2 c. brown sugar
Whipped cream

Remove core from apples and place in crock pot. Mix together all other ingredients except whipped cream. Pour over apples. Cover pot and cook on low for about 3 1/2 hours or until apples are tender. Cool and serve with whipped cream.

Baked Custard

2 cups milk, scalded
3 eggs, slightly beaten
1/3 cup sugar
1 teaspoon vanilla
1/8 teaspoon salt
Nutmeg or coconut

Scald milk, let cool slightly. Combine eggs, sugar, vanilla, and salt. Slowly stir in slightly cooled milk. Pour into buttered 1-qt baking dish. Sprinkle with nutmeg or coconut. Cover with foil. Set baking dish on a trivet or meat rack in crock pot. Pour hot water around baking dish, 1-inch deep. Cover pot and cook on high for 2 to 2 1/2 hours or until knife inserted in custard comes out clean. Serve warm or chilled. Makes 5 to 6 servings.

Baked Ham In Foil

Pour 1/2 cup water in crock-pot. Wrap precooked 3 to 4 pound ham in foil, place in crock-pot. Cover and cook on high 1 hour, then low 6 to 7 hours or until ham is hot. If desired, sprinkle ham with liquid smoke before wrapping in foil. If cooking larger ham, cook 1 hour on high then low 8 to 10 hours.

Baked Potatoes

10 to 12 potatoes
Aluminum foil

Prick potatoes with fork and wrap each in foil. Fill crock pot with potatoes. Cover and cook on low 8 to 10 hours. Do not add water.

Banana Bread

1 3/4 cup flour
2 tsp baking powder
1/4 tsp baking soda
1/2 tsp salt
1/3 c shortening
2/3 c sugar
2 eggs, well beaten
1 1/2 c banana, well mashed, overripe
1/2 c walnuts, coarsely chopped

Sift together flour, baking powder, baking soda and salt. With electric beater on low, fluff shortening in a small bowl, until soft and creamy. Add sugar gradually. Beat in eggs in a slow stream. With a fork, beat in 1/3 of the flour mixture, 1/2 the bananas another 1/3 of the flour mixture, the rest of the bananas then the last of the flour mixture. Fold in walnuts. Turn into a greased and floured baking unit or a 2 1/2 quart mold and cover. Place on a rack in crock pot. Cover crock pot, but prop the lid open with a toothpick or a twist of foil to let the excess steam escape. Cook on high for 4 to 6 hours. Cool on a rack for 10 minutes. Serve warm.

Banana Nut Bread

1/3 c shortening
1/2 c sugar
2 eggs
1-3/4 c all purpose flour

1 tsp baking powder
1/2 tsp baking soda
1/2 tsp salt
1 c mashed ripe bananas
1/2 c chopped walnuts

Cream together shortening and sugar; add eggs and beat well. Sift dry ingredients; add to creamed mixture alternately with banana, blending well after each addition. Stir in nuts. Pour into well-greased 4-6 cup mold. Cover with foil and tie a string tightly around it to keep foil down. Pour 2 cups hot water in slow-cooking pot. Place mold on rack or trivet in pot. Cover with crock pot lid and cook on high 2 to 3 hours or until bread is done. Be sure not to check bread during the first 2 hours of cooking.

Barbeque Beef Stew

2 lbs. stew meat
3 tbsp. oil
1 c. onion, sliced
1/2 c. green pepper, chopped
1 lg. clove garlic
1/2 tsp. salt
1/8 tsp. pepper
2 c. beef stock
1 cans (8 oz.) tomatoes
1 cans (4 oz.) mushrooms
1/3 c. barbecue sauce
3 tbsp. cornstarch
1/4 c. cold water

Sauté onion, pepper and garlic in oil. Add salt, pepper, beef stock, tomatoes, mushrooms and barbecue sauce. Cook in crock pot on low heat 8-10 hours. Mix cornstarch, cold water and thicken before serving. Serve over hot cooked rice.

Barbecue Brisket

First, make a batch of homemade BBQ sauce:
1 tbs liquid smoke
1 tbs crushed garlic
1 large onion chopped
2 tbs cider vinegar
1 tbs loose brown sugar
3 tbs fresh squeezed lemon juice

1-14 oz. bottle of ketchup
1/2 tsp chili powder
4 tbs Worcestershire
1 tbs dry mustard powder
1 cup water or red wine
1 tsp salt
1/8 tsp black pepper
1 tbs honey

Mix together and heat on range. Then prep the brisket by removing all silver skin if the butcher didn't already do this, place it in the crock pot, pour the homemade sauce over it and let it go on low. The length of time cooking will depend on how large a brisket you got. When done, remove lid from crock pot and using two forks shred the brisket.

Barbecue Chicken

1 chicken, cut up and skin removed
1 cup ketchup
3/4 cup brown sugar
3 tablespoons Worcestershire sauce

Place chicken in crock pot. Combine remaining ingredients and pour over chicken. Cook 4 hours on high or 8-10 hours on low.

Barbecue Chicken Breasts

4-6 pieces chicken
1 bottle BBQ sauce
1/2 cup white vinegar
1/2 cup brown sugar
1 tsp. mesquite seasoning
1/2 tsp. garlic powder
1/2-1 tsp. red pepper flakes

Mix BBQ sauce with all ingredients listed under it. Place chicken in crock pot. Pour sauce over all. Cook slowly in crock pot about 4-6 hours. Serve with baked beans, potato salad and coleslaw.

Barbecue Chicken Whole

1 frying chicken cut up or quartered
1 can condensed tomato soup
3/4 cup chopped onion

1/4 cup vinegar
3 tablespoons brown sugar
1 tablespoon Worcestershire sauce
1/2 teaspoon salt
1/4 teaspoon sweet basil
1/4 teaspoon thyme

Place chicken in crock pot. Combine all other ingredients and pour over chicken. Cover tightly and cook at "low" for 6-8 hours. Makes 4 servings.

Barbecue Pork Roast

1 pork roast (or beef)
Juice of 1 lemon
1 small onion, cut up
1 teaspoon sugar
1 bottle barbecue sauce

Cook roast covered in water in crock pot overnight on low 10-12 hours. Pour off water and pull meat into shredded pieces. Sauté onion in a little butter. Combine barbecue sauce, onions, sugar and juice of lemon with meat in crock pot and cook on high for 1 1/2 to 2 1/2 hours or on low for 3 to 6 hours.

Barbecue Pork Sandwiches

1 pork roast
1 bottle bar-b-cue sauce
About 1/2 to 1 cup water

Just throw in crock pot on high for about 6 hrs. Or low for about 10 hrs. When it's done, just remove meat from bone and serve on hamburger buns or rolls with more BBQ sauce or ketchup, etc.

Barbecue Sauce

1 cup chopped celery
1 medium onion chopped
1 tbsp. butter
Sauté until golden brown.
2 tbsp. vinegar
1 tbsp. brown sugar
3 tbsp. Worcestershire sauce
1 tbsp. lemon juice

1 tsp. salt (optional)
1 tsp. mustard
1 cup ketchup
1 cup water
2 lbs. ground beef

Combine all ingredients in a large saucepan. Cook slowly for 2 -21/2 hours.

Barbecue Steak

1 1/2 lb boneless chuck steak, 1 1/2" thick
1 clove garlic, peeled and minced
1/4 cup wine vinegar
1 tbsp brown sugar
1 tsp paprika
2 tbsp Worcestershire sauce
1/2 cup catsup (ketchup)
1 tsp salt
1 tsp dry or prepared mustard
1/4 tsp black pepper

Cut the beef on a diagonal, across the grain into slices 1" wide. Place these in the crock pot. In a small bowl, combine the remaining ingredients. Pour over the meat, and mix. Cover and cook on low for 3 to 5 hours.

Barbecued Bean Soup

1 lb great northern beans, soaked
2 tsp salt
1 med onion, chopped
1/8 tsp ground pepper
2 lb beef short ribs
6 cup water
3/4 cup barbecue sauce

Place all ingredients in crock pot except barbecue sauce cover and cook on low 10to 16 hours. Before serving, remove short ribs and cut meat from bones. Return meat to crock pot. Stir in barbecue sauce before serving.

Barbecued Cocktail Meatballs

2 lbs. lean ground beef
1 1/3 c ketchup, divided

3 t seasoned dry bread crumbs
1 egg, slightly beaten
2 t dried onion flakes
3/4 t garlic salt
1/2 t black pepper
1 c packed brown sugar
1 cans (6 oz) tomato paste
1/4 c reduced-sodium soy sauce
1/4 c cider vinegar
1 1/2 t hot pepper sauce

Preheat oven to 350 degrees. Combine ground beef, 1/3 cup ketchup, bread crumbs, egg onion flakes, garlic sale, and black pepper in medium bowl. Mix lightly but thoroughly; shape into 1-inch meatballs. Place meatballs in two 15 x 10" jelly-roll pans or shallow roasting pans. Bake 18 minutes or until browned. Transfer meatballs to crock pot. Mix remaining 1 cup ketchup, sugar, tomato paste, and soy sauce, vinegar, and hot pepper sauce in medium bowl. Pour over meatballs. Cover and cook on low 4 hours. Serve with cocktail picks. Makes about 4 dozen meatballs.

Barbecued Meatballs I

1 to 2 lbs. ground beef
2 tsp. Worcestershire sauce
2/3 c. evaporated milk
1 envelope dry onion soup mix sauce:
2 c. ketchup
1 c. brown sugar, packed
1 tbsp. Worcestershire sauce

Mix beef, 2 teaspoons Worcestershire sauce, evaporated milk and soup mix. Shape into balls the size of walnuts. Broil 4 inches from broiler for 12 minutes or until done. Turn if necessary to keep from burning. Mix sauce ingredients and boil 10 minutes. Pour over meatballs in crock pot turned on low. 2 pounds of ground beef makes about 50 meatballs.

Barbecued Meatballs II

2 pounds ground beef
1 cup bread crumbs
1 teaspoon garlic powder
2 packages onion soup mix
2 teaspoons Worcestershire sauce
2 eggs sauce:

2 onions, chopped
2 cans tomato paste (12 ounces total)
2 cloves garlic, minced
1/4 cup Worcestershire sauce
1/4 cup red wine vinegar
1/2 cup brown sugar
1/2 cup sweet pickle relish
1/2 cup beef broth
2 teaspoons salt
2 teaspoons dry mustard

Combine first 6 ingredients and mix well. Shape into meatballs and brown in a skillet with 1 tablespoon of oil. Drain on paper towels. Add all sauce ingredients to crock pot and stir well. Add meatballs and cook, covered, on low for 5 to 6 hours (high for 2 to 3). Serve from the crock pot. Makes about 60 meatballs.

Barbecued Pork Strips

1/2 cup soy sauce
1/4 cup dry sherry
1/2 cup brown sugar
2 cloves garlic, crushed
1/8 teaspoon pepper
1/2 cup barbecue sauce
1 8-ounce can pineapple chunks (do not drain)
3 pounds lean pork, cut into strips, browned, and drained

Combine all ingredients except pork strips in crock pot and stir well. Add pork and stir to coat. Cook on low, covered, for 8 to 10 hours. Serve with sauce. Makes about 15 servings.

Barbecued Ribs

4 pounds pork baby back ribs
Salt and pepper to taste
2 cups ketchup
1 cup chili sauce
1/2 cup packed brown sugar
4 tablespoons vinegar
2 teaspoons dried oregano
2 teaspoons Worcestershire sauce
1 dash hot sauce

Preheat oven to 400 degrees. Season ribs with salt and pepper. Place in a shallow baking pan. Brown in oven 15 minutes. Turn over, and brown another 15 minutes; drain fat. In a medium bowl, mix together the ketchup, chili sauce, brown sugar, vinegar, oregano, Worcestershire sauce, hot sauce, and salt and pepper. Place ribs in crock pot. Pour sauce over ribs, and turn to coat. Cover, and cook on low 6 to 8 hours, or until ribs are tender.

Barley With Mushrooms & Green Onions

1 cup barley
1 can (14 1/2 oz) roasted garlic chicken broth (about 2 cups)
3 green onions, thinly sliced (about 1/2 cup)
4 to 6 ounces fresh or canned mushrooms, sliced
Salt or seasoned salt and pepper to taste
2 teaspoons butter or margarine

Combine all ingredients in crock pot. Cover and cook on low for 4 to 4 1/2 hours.

Bavarian Red Cabbage

1 large head of red cabbage, washed and coarsely sliced
2 medium onions coarsely chopped
6 tart apples, cored & quartered
2 tsp. salt
2 cups hot water
3 tbsp sugar
2/3 cup cider vinegar
6 tbsp bacon grease or butter

Place all ingredients in the crock pot in order listed. Cover and cook on low 8 to 10 hours. Stir well before serving.

Bayou Gumbo

3 tablespoons Pillsbury best all purpose flour
3 tablespoons oil
1/2 pound smoked sausage, cut into 1/2 inch slices
2 cups frozen cut okra
1 large onion, chopped
1 large green bell pepper, chopped
3 garlic cloves, minced
1/4 teaspoon ground red pepper (cayenne)
1/4 teaspoon pepper
1 (14.5 ounce) can diced tomatoes, undrained

1 (12-ounce) package frozen shelled deveined cooked medium shrimp, rinsed
1 1/2 cups uncooked regular long-grain white rice
3 cups water

In small saucepan, combine flour and oil; mix well. Cook, stirring constantly, over medium-high heat for 5 minutes. Reduce heat to medium; cook, stirring constantly, about 10 minutes or until mixture turns reddish brown. Place flour-oil mixture in 3 1/2 to 4 quart crock pot. Stir in all remaining ingredients except shrimp, rice and water. Cover; cook on low setting for 7-9 hours. When ready to serve, cook rice in water as directed on package. Meanwhile, add shrimp to gumbo mixture in crock pot; mix well. Cover; cook on low setting for additional 20 minutes. Serve gumbo over rice. Makes 6 servings.

BBQ Chicken Wings

5 lbs. chicken wings, with tips cut off
1 (12 oz.) bottle chili sauce
1/3 c. lemon juice
1 tbsp. Worcestershire sauce
2 tbsp. molasses
2 tsp. salt
2 tsp. chili powder
1/4 tsp. hot pepper sauce

Dash of garlic salt place wings in crock pot. Combine all remaining ingredients and pour over chicken. Cook on low 6 to 8 hours or on high for 2 to 3 hours. Makes 6 to 8 servings.

Bean Soup

1/2 bag northern beans (dry)
4 c. water
2 (8 oz.) cans tomato sauce
Lawry's season
Salt
Pepper
2 med. potatoes, diced
2 carrots, shredded
2 sm. onions, diced
Ham, diced

Soak beans overnight in enough water to cover. Drain beans, put in crock pot and add all other ingredients. Stir. Cook on low all day.

Beef Burgundy

2 lb. stew beef, 1" cubes
1 1/2 lg. onion, sliced
1 clove garlic, minced
1/2 c. catsup
2 tbsp. Worcestershire sauce
2 tbsp. brown sugar
2 tsp. salt
2 tsp. paprika
1/2 tsp. dry mustard
1 pound mushrooms
½ cup water
½ cup burgundy wine

Mix beef, onion, garlic, catsup, Worcestershire sauce, sugar, salt, paprika and mustard in crock pot with 1/2 c. water and 1/2 c. burgundy wine. Cook on low 8 hours. Thicken with some flour. Add 1 pound fresh mushrooms for 6 hours of cooking.

Beef And Rice Casserole

1 lb. hamburger, browned & drained
1 sm. onion, sliced very thin
1/2 c. celery, sliced
1 tsp. soy sauce
1/8 tsp. oregano
1 can cream of chicken soup
1 c. rice, cooked
Almonds (optional)

Combine cooked beef and all other ingredients except rice and almonds in cooker. Cook on high for 3 hours. Add rice and serve with toasted almonds (optional). Makes 6 servings.

Beer Meatballs

1 can of beer
1 6 oz can spicy v-8 juice
1 tsp. lemon juice
1 tsp. hot sauce
1/2 c. Italian bread crumbs
1 c. onions
Salt and pepper to taste
1 lg. bottle ketchup
1 tsp. horseradish

1 tsp. Worcestershire sauce
2 to 3 lbs. ground beef
2 to 3 eggs

Combine ground beef, 1/2 cup onions, Italian bread crumbs, eggs. Make the mixture into small meatballs. Then fry or bake the meat. In saucepan combine remaining ingredients. Simmer for 15 minutes. Put meatballs and sauce into crock pot/Crockpot. The sauce should cover the meat. Allow to simmer in crock pot for at least 3 hours, however, the longer you let them simmer, the better they are! 6 to 10 hours on low temperature is great. Stir them occasionally.

Best Dip Ever

1 (1 pound) package Velveeta
1 cans chili - no beans
1 pound medium or spicy sausage, browned and crumbled

Put it in the crock pot on low until blended and then serve.

Black Bean Chili

1 pound dry black beans
2 tsp oil 6 garlic cloves, minced or pressed
2 onions, chopped
1/4 tsp crushed red pepper flakes
1 tsp chili powder
1 tsp ground cumin
1 tsp dried oregano
1 bay leaf
1 28 oz. can chopped tomatoes in juice
1 tsp soy sauce
2 c water
6 oz. can tomato paste
1 tsp red wine vinegar
2 cans beans (pinto, garbanzo, great northern, etc.)--drained and rinsed
Garnishes: grated cheese, sour cream, chopped parsley, onion, etc.

Rinse and sort the beans and place in the crock pot with a generous amount of water. Cook on low overnight (no presoaking necessary). In the morning drain the cooking water. Heat the oil in a skillet and sauté the onions, garlic and red pepper flakes. Cook 1 minute, then add chili powder and cumin and cook 2 minutes, stirring. Add this mixture to the crock pot along with all remaining ingredients except canned beans and garnishes. Stir well and cook on low all day. Stir in canned beans an hour or so before serving. Serve with garnishes.

Black Bean Soup

2 onion, chopped
2 cloves garlic, minced
3 tablespoons butter
1 pound black beans, soaked overnight, drained
1 ham bone, cracked
1 stalk celery, chopped
1 bay leaf
1/2 cup sherry or dry white wine
Salt and pepper, to taste

Sauté onions and garlic in butter until transparent. Combine with beans, ham bone, celery, bay leaf, and 2 quarts water in the crock pot. Cook on high, covered for 2hours, then on low for 8 to 10 hours. Remove ham bone and bay leaf. Puree soup and return to pot. Add sherry, salt and pepper and heat through. Serve in soup bowls garnished with chopped hard-boiled eggs, parsley, and lemon slices.

Boiled Peanuts

1 1/2 quarts green uncooked peanuts
1/2 cup salt
2 1/2 quarts water

Wash peanuts until water runs clear. Put clean peanuts in crockery pot, add salt and water; stir. Cook, covered, on high for 5 to 7 hours. Add additional water during cooking, if necessary, to keep peanuts covered.

Breakfast Cobbler

4 medium-sized apples -- peeled and sliced
1/4 cup honey
1 tsp cinnamon
2 tablespoons butter -- melted
2 cups granola cereal

Place apples in crock pot and mix in remaining ingredients. Cover and cook on low 7-9 hours (overnight) or on high 2-3 hours. Serve with milk. Makes 4 servings

broccoli & cheese soup

2 c. cooked noodles
1 (10 oz.) pkg. frozen chopped broccoli, thawed
3 tbsp. chopped onions
2 tbsp. butter
1 tbsp. flour
2 cups shredded American cheese
Salt to taste
5 1/2 c. milk

Combine all ingredients in crock pot. Stir well. Cook on low for 4 hours. 8 servings.

Broccoli Cheese Dip

2 (10 oz.) boxes of frozen chopped broccoli
2 cans cream of mushroom soup
1/4 c. sour cream
1/2 lb. Mexican Velveeta cheese
1/2 lb. reg. Velveeta cheese
1 tbsp. garlic salt

Cook and drain broccoli. Melt cheese in crock pot. Mix soups, sour cream, broccoli and garlic salt. Mix into melted cheese. Serve as dip with tortilla chips.

Broccoli Dip

1 pkg. (10oz) frozen chopped broccoli
2 ribs celery, chopped
1 med. white onion, chopped
3/4 stick margarine
2 rolls garlic cheese
1 can cream of mushroom soup
1 med. can mushroom pieces
1 can sliced water chestnuts
2 tsp. Worcestershire sauce

Cook broccoli until tender. Sauté celery and onion in oleo until tender. Place broccoli and sautéed vegetables in crock pot; add mushrooms, cheese, cream of mushroom soup. Stir well and heat on low until cheese is melted. Add water chestnuts and Worcestershire sauce. Serve warm in the crock pot, with chips or crackers.

Broccoli Soufflé

2 pkgs. frozen chopped broccoli (2 lbs.)
1 can cream of celery soup (undiluted)
1 c. real mayonnaise
3 tbsp. grated onion
2 eggs, beaten
1 c. grated cheddar cheese
Ritz crackers
1 stick melted margarine

Cook broccoli; drain and cool. Mix soup, mayonnaise, onion, egg, and cheese and add to cooled broccoli. Put in a lightly greased 3 1/2-quart crockery cooker. Mix 1 stacks Ritz or buttery crackers (crushed) with margarine or butter. Put on top. Cook on high for 2 to 3 hours.

Brunswick Stew

1 chicken, 3 lbs, cut up
2 quarts water
1 onion, chopped
2 cups ham; cooked, cubed
3 potatoes, diced
2 cans tomatoes; 16 oz, ea, cut up
10 ounces lima beans, frozen and thawed
10 ounces corn; whole kernel, frozen, partially thawed
2 teaspoons salt
1 teaspoon sugar
1/4 teaspoon pepper
1/2 teaspoon seasoned salt

In a crock pot combine chicken with water, onion, ham, and potatoes. Cook covered on low for 4 to 5 hours or until chicken is done. Lift chicken out of pot; remove meat from bones. Return chicken meat to pot. Add tomatoes, beans, corn, salt, seasoned salt, sugar and pepper. Cover and cook on high 1 hour. Makes 8 servings.

Cajun Brew Pork N Beans

5 cans pork-n-beans (2nd to smallest size)
2 8oz cans tomato sauce
2 onions (chopped)
6 hot links (sliced)
1/4 bottle barbeque sauce (average size)

Worcestershire sauce
Hot sauce
Cajun seasonings
Liquid smoke
Mustard
Brown sugar

Mix all ingredients in a crock pot and crank it up to high. Let it cook all day, stirring occasionally. Can also be made on the stove top, but let it simmer for several hours stirring occasionally.

Cajun Pecans

1 pound pecan halves
4 tbs butter, melted
1 tbs chili powder
1 tsp salt
1 tsp dried basil
1 tsp dried oregano
1 tsp dried thyme
1/2 tsp onion powder
1/4 tsp garlic powder
1/4 tsp cayenne pepper

Combine all ingredients in crock pot. Cover and cook on high for 15 minutes. Turn on low, uncovered, stirring occasionally for 2 hours. Transfer nuts to a baking sheet and cool completely.

Camp Stew

1 cans BBQ beef
1 cans BBQ chicken
1 cans BBQ pork
1 cans stewed tomatoes
1 can corn
3 c. cubed potatoes
1 onion, chopped

Cube potatoes, chopped onion. Cook until partly tender. Place in crock pot/Crockpot. Open all cans and add to crock pot, stir. Cook for at least an hour. Serve with corn sticks or bread sticks.

Candied Bananas

6 green-tipped bananas, peeled
1/2 cup flaked coconut
1/2 tsp cinnamon
1/4 tsp salt
1/2 cup dark corn syrup
1/4 cup butter or margarine, melted
2 tsp grated lemon peel
1/4 cup lemon juice

Put bananas and coconut into large enough crock pot to fit in single layer. Sprinkle with cinnamon and salt. Mix corn syrup, butter, lemon peel, and lemon juice; pour over bananas. Cover and cook on low 1 to 2 hours.

Cannellini A La Catania

1 lb dried cannellini beans (white kidney beans) use white northern if unable to find cannellini
6 c water
2 hot Italian sausages, sliced
1 lg onion, chopped
1 lg garlic clove, minced
2 lg tomatoes, ripe, peeled and coarsely chopped
1 bay leaf, crumbled
1/2 tsp thyme, crumbled
1/2 tsp basil, crumbled
3 strips of orange rind (1in)
1 tsp salt
1/4 tsp pepper
1 tsp instant beef broth

Pick over beans and rinse. Cover beans with water in a large kettle; bring to boiling; cover; cook 2 minutes; remove from heat; let stand 1 hour. Pour into an electric crock pot. brown sausages in a small skillet; push to one side; sauté onion and garlic in same pan until soft; stir in tomato, bay leaf, thyme, basil, orange strips, salt and pepper and instant beef broth; bring to boiling; stir into beans; cover. Cook on low for 10 hours or on high for 5 hours or until beans are tender. Yield: 6 servings

Caramel Nut Rolls

2 8 oz. pkgs. refrigerator biscuits
1/4 c. melted butter or margarine

1/2 c. brown sugar
1/4 c. chopped nuts
Cinnamon

Mix brown sugar and nuts together. Dip each refrigerator biscuit in melted butter, then brown sugar and nuts. Place in rival bread and cake pan or a 3 pound coffee can. Sprinkle each layer of biscuits with cinnamon. If using coffee can, cover with several layers of paper towels. Cook on high for 3-4 hours.

Caramel Rum Fondue

7 ounces caramels
1/4 cup miniature marshmallows
1/3 cup whipping cream
2 teaspoons rum or 1/4 tsp rum extract

Combine caramels and cream in crock pot. Cover and heat until melted, 30 to 60 minutes. Stir in marshmallows and rum. Cover and continue cooking 30 minutes. Serve with apple wedges or pound cake.

Carmel Apples

2 packages (14oz) bags caramels
1/4 cup water
8 medium apples

In crock pot, combine caramels and water. Cover and cook on high for 1to 1 1/2 hours, stirring frequently. Wash and dry apples. Insert stick into stem end of each apple. Turn control on low. Dip apple into hot caramel and turn to coat entire surface. Holding apple above pot, scrape off excess accumulation of caramel from bottom apple. Place on greased wax paper to cool.

Carrot Pudding

4 large carrots, cooked and grated
1 small onion, grated
1/2 teaspoon salt
1/4 teaspoon nutmeg
1 tablespoon sugar
1 cup milk
3 eggs, beaten

Mix together carrots, onion, salt, nutmeg, sugar, milk, and eggs. Pour into crock pot and cook on high for 3-4 hours.

Casserole In The Cooker

1 package (16 oz) frozen broccoli cuts, thawed and drained
3 cp cubed fully cooked ham
1 cans condensed cream of mushroom soup, undiluted
1 jar (8 oz) process cheese sauce
1 cp milk
1 cp uncooked instant rice
1 celery rib, chopped
1 small onion, chopped

In a crock pot, combine broccoli and ham. Combine the soup, cheese sauce, milk, rice, celery and onion; stir into the broccoli mixture. Cover and cook on low 4-5 hours or until rice is tender. 4 servings.

Cheddar Potato Slices

1 can (10 3/4 ounces) Campbell's® condensed cream of mushroom soup
1/2 teaspoon paprika
1/2 teaspoon pepper
4 medium baking potatoes (about 1 1/4 pounds), sliced 1/4-inch thick
1 cup shredded cheddar cheese (4 ounces)

Mix soup, paprika and pepper. In greased 2-quart shallow baking dish arrange potatoes in overlapping rows. Sprinkle with cheese. Spoon soup mixture over cheese. Cover and bake at 400°f. For 45 minutes. Uncover and bake 10 minutes more or until potatoes are tender. Serves 6.

Cheese And Potato Casserole

2 lb. pkg. frozen hash brown potatoes (partially thawed)
2 (10 oz.) cans cheddar cheese soup
1 (13 oz.) can evaporated milk
1 can French fried onion rings, divided
Salt and pepper to taste

Combine potatoes, soup, milk, and half the can of onion rings; pour into greased crock pot and add salt and pepper. Cover and cook on low for 8 to 9 hours or high for 4 hours. Sprinkle the rest of the onion rings of top before serving.

Cheese & Artichoke Dip

8 ounces process American cheese

1 cans (10oz) 98% fat-free cream of mushroom soup

2 teaspoons Worcestershire sauce

1/4 cup evaporated milk

1 teaspoon dry mustard

1 1/2 cups shredded cheddar cheese

1/3 cup chopped roasted red pepper

1 cans artichoke hearts, drained and coarsely chopped

Combine all ingredients in the crock pot. Cover and cook on low for 2 to 3 hours, until melted. Stir well and serve with assorted crackers, bread cubes, or chips.

Cheesy Cauliflower And Broccoli

1 (10 oz) pkg frozen cauliflower, thawed

1 (10 oz) pkg frozen broccoli, thawed

1 cans cheddar cheese soup

4 slices bacon

Salt and pepper to taste

1/4 cup shredded cheddar cheese, if desired

Fry bacon until crisp; drain well on paper towels then crumble. Place broccoli and cauliflower in crockery pot. Top with soup, sprinkle with bacon. Season with salt and pepper. Cover and cook on low for 4 to 5 hours. About 20 minutes before done, top with cheddar cheese if used. Serves 6 to 8.

Cheesy Crockpot Chicken

3 whole boneless chicken breasts

2 cans cream chicken soup

1 cans cheddar cheese soup

Remove all fat and skin from chicken; rinse and pat dry, sprinkle with salt, pepper and garlic powder. Put in Crockpot and add the three soups straight from the cans. Cook on low all day (at least 8 hrs) does not lift the lid. Serve over rice or noodles.

Cheesy Crockpot Chicken II

6 chicken breasts (boneless & skinless)

Salt & pepper to taste

Garlic powder, to taste

2 cans cream of chicken soup
1 cans cheddar cheese soup

Rinse chicken and sprinkle with salt, pepper and garlic powder. Mix undiluted soup and pour over chicken in the crock pot. Cook on low 6 to 8 hours. Serve over rice or noodles.

Cheesy Crockpot Chicken And Vegetables

1/3 c. diced Canadian bacon or ham
2-3 carrots, sliced or chopped
2-3 celery ribs, sliced or chopped
1 small onion, sliced or chopped
2 cans mushrooms or 1/4 lb fresh, sliced
1 can green beans, drained very well
1/4 c. water

Layer in crock pot in order given.
2-3 lbs. chicken, cut up. Put on top of veggies, largest pieces first.
2 tsp. chicken bouillon granules
1 tbs. chopped fresh parsley
3/4 tsp. poultry seasoning

Mix together and sprinkle over chicken pieces.
1 can condensed cheddar cheese soup
1 tbs. flour 1/4 c. parmesan cheese

Mix together and drop on top of chicken, do not stir. Cover and cook on high 3-4 hours, or low 6-8 hours.

Cherry Cobbler

1 16 oz can cherry pie filling, light
1 pkg cake mix for 1 layer cake or sweet muffin mix
1 egg
3 tablespoons evaporated milk
1/2 teaspoon cinnamon
1/2 cup chopped nuts, optional

Put pie filling in lightly buttered 3 1/2-quart crock pot and cook on high for 30 minutes. Mix together the remaining ingredients and spoon onto the hot pie filling. Cover and cook for 2 to

3 hours on low. You may also use a lightly greased soufflé dish in a larger crock pot. 6 servings.

Cherry Crisp

1 can (21 oz) cherry pie filling
2/3 cup brown sugar
1/2 cup quick-cooking oats
1/2 cup flour
1 teaspoon brown sugar
1/3 cup butter, softened

Lightly butter a 3 1/2-quart crock pot. Place cherry pie filling in the crock pot. Combine dry ingredients and mix well; cut in butter with a pastry cutter or fork. Sprinkle crumbs over the cherry pie filling. Cook for 5 hours on low.

Chicken A La King

1 1/2 to 2 pounds boneless chicken tenders
1 to 1 1/2 cup matchstick-cut carrots
1 bunch green onions (scallions) sliced in 1/2-inch pieces
1 jar Kraft pimiento or pimiento & olive process cheese spread (5oz)
1 cans 98% fat-free cream of chicken soup
2 tablespoons dry sherry (optional)
Salt and pepper to taste

Put all ingredients in the crock pot (3 1/2-quart or larger) in the order given; stir to combine. Cover and cook on low for 7 to 9 hours. Serve over rice, toast, or biscuits. Serves 6 to 8.

Chicken Cacciatore In Crockpot

Place cut up chicken in crock pot, cover with one large undrained can of cut-up tomatoes, one cut-up onion, one cut-up green pepper, minced garlic (to taste), one tbs. Italian herbs, red pepper flakes to taste. Cook all on low 6-8 hours until falling apart.

Chicken Casserole

1 8oz pkg noodles
3 cups diced cooked chicken
1/2 cup diced celery
1/2 cup diced green pepper
1/2 cup diced onion
1 4 oz can mushrooms

1 4 oz jar pimiento
1/2 cup parmesan cheese
1 1/2 cups cream style cottage cheese
1 cup grated sharp process cheese
1 can cream of chicken soup
1/2 cup chicken broth
2 tbsp. melted butter
1/2 tsp. basil

Cook noodles according to pkg and drain and rinse thoroughly. In a large bowl, combine remaining ingredients with noodles until well mixed. Pour mixture into greased Crockpot. Cover and cook on low for 6-8 hours or high 3-4 hours. Serves 6

Chicken Chili

2 whole chicken breasts, skinned,
Deboned, cut in 1/2" chunks
Celery heart
1 med. onion
2 cans stewed tomatoes, sliced
16 oz. med. salsa or picante sauce
1 cans chick peas (or 1 pkg. pkg. white kidney beans)
6 oz. mushrooms
Olive oil

Brown chicken in 1 tablespoon olive oil. Chop celery, onion and mushrooms. Combine all ingredients in large crock pot, stir and simmer on low heat for 6-8 hours. Serve with bread or taco chips.

Chicken

1 frying chicken, cut up
Salt & pepper
1 can cream of mushroom soup
1/2 c. sauterne or sherry
2 tbsp. butter or margarine, melted
2 tbsp. dry Italian salad dressing mix
2 (3 oz.) pkgs. cream cheese, cut in cubes
1 tbsp. onion, chopped

Wash chicken and pat dry. Brush with butter. Sprinkle with salt and pepper. Place in crock pot. Sprinkle with dry salad mix. Cover and cook on low for 5 to 6 hours. About 3/4 hour before serving, mix soup, cream cheese, wine, and onion in small saucepan. Cook until smooth. Pour over chicken in pot. Cover and cook for 30 minutes on low. Serve with sauce. Serve with rice or noodles. Serves 4 to 6.

Chicken And Dressing

1 stick butter
1 c. chopped onions
1 c. chopped celery
1 pan cornbread (crumbled)
6 slices bread (crumbled)
1/4 lb. crackers (crumbled)
2 tsp. thyme, sage or poultry seasoning
4 c. chicken broth
1 (14 oz.) can chicken broth
4 eggs (beaten)
1/2 c. milk
1/2 tsp. baking powder
3 to 4 c. chicken

Boil hen or large fryer for your broth and chicken. Sauté onions and celery in butter. Pour this mixture over bread crumbs in a very large mixing bowl. Add seasonings and toss together. Pour enough broth into mixture to moisten. Add beaten eggs and mix together well. Add baking powder, milk, and remaining broth. Mixture should be very slushy. (Pouring point). Add chicken. Pack tightly into a 5 quart crock pot cover and cook on high for 1 hour. Reduce to low and cook 4 to 8 hours.

Chicken And Dumplings

1 (3 lb.) chicken, cut up
1/2 c. chicken bouillon broth
2 tsp. salt
1/2 tsp. pepper
1/2 tsp. poultry seasoning
3 stalks celery, cut in
1 inch pieces
3 sm. carrots cut into
1 inch pieces
2 c. packaged biscuit mix
3/4 c. milk
1 tsp. parsley flakes

Wash chicken pieces; cut away excess fat. Place raw chicken pieces in crock with largest bony pieces on bottom. Add bouillon broth; sprinkle chicken with salt, pepper, poultry seasoning. Add celery and carrots on top. Cover. Place crock into outer shell; cook. for 3 1/2 quart: cook on low setting, 8 to 10 hours or high setting 4 to 4 1/2 hours. for 5 1/2 quart: cook on low setting, 6 to 8 hours or high setting, 3 to 3 1/2 hours. Combine biscuit mix, milk, parsley flakes; stir until just moistened. Drop dumpling mixture by spoonfuls (about 8) over steaming chicken; cover, cook on high setting 30 minutes in 3 1/2 quart; 15 to 20 minutes in 5 1/2 quart. (Do not remove the cover during the steaming of the dumplings). Serve immediately - when dumplings are at their best. Makes 4 servings.

Chicken In Mushroom Gravy

3 whole chicken breasts, halved
1/4 c. dry white wine or chicken broth
1 can cream of chicken soup
1 (4 oz.) can mushrooms, sliced
Salt & pepper

Place chicken pieces in crock pot. Season with salt and pepper. Mix wine and soup. Pour over chicken. Add mushrooms. Cover and cook on low for 7 to 9 hours or high 3 to 4 hours. Recipe may be doubled in 5-quart crock pot.

Chicken Merlot With Mushrooms

2 1/2 to 3 lbs. meaty chicken pieces, skinned
3 c. sliced fresh mushrooms
1 large onion, chopped
2 cloves garlic, minced
3/4 c. chicken broth
1 6-ounce cans tomato paste
1/4 c. dry red wine (such as merlot) or chicken broth
2 tbsp. quick-cooking tapioca
2 tbsp. snipped fresh basil or 1 1/2 tsp. dried basil, crushed
2 tsp. sugar
1/4 tsp. salt
1/4 tsp. pepper
2 c. hot cooked noodles
2 tbsp. finely shredded parmesan
Rinse chicken; set aside.

In a 3 1/2-4-or 5-quart crockery cooker place mushrooms, onion, and garlic. Place chicken pieces on top of the vegetables. In a bowl combine broth, tomato paste, wine or chicken broth, tapioca, dried basil (if using), sugar, salt, and pepper. Pour over all. Cover; cook on low-heat setting for 7 to 8 hours or on high-heat setting for 3 1/2 to 4 hours. If using, stir in fresh basil. To serve, spoon chicken, mushroom mixture, and sauce over hot cooked noodles sprinkle with parmesan cheese. Makes 4 to 6 servings.

Chicken Or Turkey Pie

3 cups diced cooked chicken or turkey
2 cans (14 1/2 ounce each) chicken broth
1/2 teaspoon salt
1/2 teaspoon pepper
1 stalk celery, thinly sliced
1 medium onion, chopped
1 bay leaf
3 cups potatoes, peeled and cubed
1 package frozen mixed veggies (16 oz)
1 cup milk
1 cup flour
1 teaspoon pepper
1/2 teaspoon salt
1 9-inch refrigerated pie crust

In crock pot, combine chicken, broth, 1/2 teaspoon salt, 1/2 teaspoon pepper, celery, onion, bay leaf, potatoes, and mixed vegetables. Cover and cook on low 8 to 10 hours or on high 4 to 6 hours. Remove bay leaf. Pre heat oven to 400 degrees. In a small bowl, mix milk and flour. Gradually stir flour and water mixture into crock pot. Stir in pepper, poultry seasoning, and salt/ remove the liner from crock pot base and carefully place 9-inch pie crust over the mixture. Place the crockery liner inside pre-heated oven and bake (uncovered) for about 15 minutes, or until browned. If your liner is not removable, put the mixture in a casserole dish, cover with the pie crust and bake as above. Serves 8.

Chicken Soup

2 onions, chopped
3 carrots, sliced
2 stalks celery, sliced
2 teaspoons salt
1/4 teaspoon pepper
1/2 teaspoon basil
1/4 teaspoon leaf thyme

3 tablespoons dry parsley flakes
1 package frozen peas (10 oz.)
1 2-1/2 to 3 lb. whole fryer
4 cups water or chicken stock
1 cup noodles

Place all ingredients in crock pot, except noodles, in order listed. Cover and cook on low 8 to 10 hours, or high 4 to 6 hours. One hour before serving, remove chicken and cool slightly. Remove meat from bones and return meat to crock pot. Add noodles. Turn to high. Cover and cook 1 hour.

Chicken Wings In BBQ Sauce

3 pounds chicken wings (16 wings)
Salt and pepper to taste
1 1/2 cups any variety barbecue sauce
1/4 cup honey
2 teaspoons prepared mustard or spicy mustard
2 teaspoons Worcestershire sauce
Tabasco to taste, optional

Rinse chicken and pat dry. Cut off and discard wing tips. Cut each wing at joint to make two sections. Sprinkle wing parts with salt and pepper. Place wings on a broiler pan. Broil 4-5 inches from the heat for 20 minutes, 10 minutes for each side or until chicken is brown. Transfer chicken to crock pot. For sauce, combine barbecue sauce, honey, mustard, Worcestershire sauce and if more heat is desired...Tabasco to taste in a small mixing bowl. Pour over chicken wings. Cover and cook on low for 4-5 hours or on high 2 -2 1/2 hours. Serve directly from crock pot. Makes about 32 appetizers.

Chicken Wings In Teriyaki Sauce

3 pounds chicken wings (16 wings)
1 large onion, chopped
1 cup soy sauce
1 cup brown sugar
2 teaspoons ground ginger
2 cloves garlic, minced
1/4 cup dry cooking sherry

Rinse chicken and pat dry. Cut off and discard wing tips. Cut each wing at joint to make two sections. Place wing parts on broiler pan. Broil 4-5 inches from the heat for 20 minutes, 10 minutes for each side or until chicken is brown. Transfer chicken to crock pot. Mix together onion, soy sauce, brown sugar, ginger, garlic and cooking sherry in bowl. Pour over chicken wings. Cover and cook on low 5-6 hours or on high 2-3 hours. Stir chicken wings once to ensure wings are evenly coated with sauce. Serve from crock pot. Makes about 32 pieces

Chili

2 lbs. ground beef
1 lg. onion
1 lg. green pepper
1 lg. jalapeno pepper
Chili powder to taste
Garlic salt to taste
Salt to taste
Pepper to taste
Sugar to taste
2 cans crushed tomatoes
1 cans tomato puree
1 cans kidney beans
2 cans chili hot beans

Brown beef. Sauté chopped onion and green pepper in grease. Mix beef, onion and green pepper. Add spices; let stand 1 hour. Add tomatoes, tomato puree, beans; cook in crock pot all day. Best if refrigerated and warmed the next day.

Chili Beef Dip

1 (11 oz.) can condensed chili beef soup
3 oz. pkg. cream cheese, softened
1/2 cup sour cream
1 tbsp. water
1 teaspoon prepared mustard
1 teaspoon Worcestershire sauce
1/2 teaspoon chili sauce
1/4 teaspoon hot pepper sauce, optional

In crock pot, combine all ingredients; mix well. Cover and cook on low for 1 1/2 to 2 hours, stirring occasionally, or until cheese is melted and dip is hot. Serve warm with tortilla or corn chips. Makes 2 cups.

Chili Cheese Taco Dip

1 lb. hamburger
1 cans chili (no beans)

1 lb. mild Mexican Velveeta cheese, cubed or shredded

Brown hamburger; drain and place in crock pot. Add chili and cheese; cover and cook on low until cheese is melted, about 1 to 1 1/2 hours, stirring occasionally to blend ingredients. Serve warm with taco or tortilla chips.

Chili Chicken

3 whole chicken breasts (1 1/2 to 2 lbs, cut in 1 inch pieces)
1 cup chopped onion
1 cup chopped bell pepper
2 garlic cloves
2 tbsp. vegetable oil
2 cans Mexican stewed tomatoes (16 ounce each)
1 cans chili beans
2/3 cup picante sauce
1 teaspoon. chili powder
1 teaspoon. cumin
1/2 teaspoon. salt

Sauté chicken, onion, pepper, garlic in vegetable oil until vegetables are wilted. Transfer to crock pot and add remaining ingredients. Cook, covered, on low, for 4 to 6 hours. Serve over rice. Serves 4 to 6.

Chili Con Queso

2 tablespoons butter
1 medium onion, chopped
1 can jalapeno peppers, chopped
1 15 1/2 oz. tomatoes, chopped, undrained
1 jar pimiento, chopped, drained
3/4 cup cheddar cheese, grated
Salt and pepper, to taste

Sauté onion in butter in medium saucepan. Combine next 3 ingredients with onion. Heat to boiling, let simmer for 10 - 15 minutes to meld the flavors. Add cheese, mixing thoroughly until melted. Serve immediately.

Chili Dip

1 lg. jar (16oz) picante sauce, mild
2 cans refried beans
8 ounces sour cream

1/2 tsp. chili powder
1 lb. ground beef
1 onion, chopped
Salt and pepper to taste
8 oz. cheddar cheese, shredded
Jalapenos or mild chile, chopped, to taste

Cook ground beef with onion; drain. Mix everything together in crock pot and cook slowly. Serve with favorite vegetables or chips.

Chinese Beef And Pea Pods

1 to 1 1/2 lb. family steak, thinly sliced, sm. chunks
1 can beef consommé soup
1/4 c. soy sauce
1/4 tsp. ground ginger
1 bunch green onions (about 8)
2 tbsp. cornstarch
2 tbsp. water
1 can sliced water chestnuts, drained
1 sm. cans bamboo shoots, drained
1 sm. can bean sprouts, drained
1 (7 oz.) pkg. frozen Chinese pea pods, partially thawed

Combine steak in crock pot with consommé, soy sauce, ginger and onion. Cover and cook on low for 5 to 7 hours. Turn control to high. Stir in cornstarch that has been dissolved in the 2 tablespoons cold water. Cook on high for 15 minutes or until thickened. During last 5 minutes of cooking, add water chestnuts, bamboo shoots, bean sprouts and pea pods. Serve over hot rice. Serves about 6.

Chocolate Amaretto Cheesecake

Crust:
3/4 cup wafer-cookie or graham cracker crumbs
1/8 teaspoon almond extract
1 tablespoon sugar
3 tablespoons butter, melted

Filling:
1 cup ricotta cheese (light)
12 ounces cream cheese, light (Neufchatel)
1 cup sugar
2 eggs
3 tablespoons whipping cream

1/4 cup amaretto
1/4 cup plus 1 tablespoon cocoa
1/4 cup all-purpose flour
1 teaspoon vanilla
1/3 cup semi-sweet chocolate mini-morsels

Combine crust ingredients and pat into a 7-inch spring form pan. Beat the cheeses with the sugar until smooth; add eggs and whipping cream and beat for about 3 minutes on medium speed of an electric hand-held mixer. Add amaretto, cocoa, flour and vanilla; beat for about 1 more minute. Stir in semi-sweet chocolate morsels; pour into prepared pan. Place the cheesecake on a rack in the crock pot (or use a "ring" of aluminum foil to keep it off the bottom of the pot). Cover and cook on high for 2 1/2 to 3 hours. Let stand in the covered pot (after turning it off) for about 1 to 2 hours, until cool enough to handle. Cool thoroughly before removing pan sides. Chill before serving; store leftovers in the refrigerator.

Chocolate Brownie Pudding Cake

1/2 cup brown sugar
3/4 cup water
2 tbsp cocoa
2 1/2 cups brownie mix (half of a 21.5oz pkg)
1 egg
1/4 cup peanut butter
1 tablespoon soft margarine
1/4 cup water
1/4 to 1/2 cup milk chocolate chips, if desired

Combine 3/4 cup water, brown sugar, and cocoa in a saucepan. Bring to a boil. In the meantime combine the remaining ingredients in a small bowl. Whisk together or mix well with a spoon. Spread the batter evenly in the bottom of a lightly buttered crock pot. Pour boiling mixture over the batter. Cover and cook on high about 2 hours; turn heat off and let stand for about 30 minutes. Spoon into dessert dishes while warm; serve with whipped cream or ice cream. Serves 6 to 8.

Chocolate Chip Peanut Butter Cake

1/2 cup butter
1/2 cup sugar
1/2 cup brown sugar
3 eggs, beaten
1/2 cup peanut butter
3/4 cup light sour cream

1 teaspoon vanilla extract

2 1/2 cups all-purpose flour

1 teaspoon baking powder

1 teaspoon baking soda

1/2 teaspoon salt

1 cup chocolate chips

Cream butter and sugars. Beat eggs in well. Mix in peanut butter, sour cream, and vanilla. Combine flour, baking powder, soda and salt together and add to creamed mixture. Stir in most of the chocolate chips, reserving a few for the top. Spoon mixture into a greased and floured 2 1/2 to 3-quart soufflé dish or mold. Place a small trivet (or fashion a little "ring" from aluminum foil) in the crock pot, place the dish on the trivet, and then cover the dish with 4 layers of paper towels. Cover loosely to allow steam to escape and cook on high for about 4 hours. Test with a toothpick for doneness. Cool in pot until dish is cool enough to handle, and then transfer to a wire rack to cool completely.

Chocolate Peanut Butter Cake

2 c. chocolate cake mix

1/2 c. water

1/3 c. creamy peanut butter

1/2 c. chopped nuts

Combine all ingredients in bowl mixing well. Beat about 2 minutes. Pour batter into greased and floured 2 pound coffee can. Place can in Crockpot. Cover top of can with 8 paper towels. Cover Crockpot and bake on high 2 to 3 hours.

Chops In A Crock

6 pork chops, browned

1 onion, chopped

3 t. catsup

10.5 oz can cream of mushroom soup

2 t Worcestershire sauce

Place into Crockpot and simmer about 4-5 hours. Serve with rice, noodles or potatoes.

Christmas Bread Pudding

9 slices whole wheat bread 8 slices white bread

3 egg yolks, beaten

1 1/2 cups light cream

2/3 cup dark raisins

1/3 cup whole candied red cherries, halved
3/4 cup cream sherry
1 cup -water
2 egg yolks, beaten
1/4 cup powdered sugar, sifted
2 tablespoons cream sherry
1/3 cup sugar
Dash salt
1 1/2 teaspoons vanilla
2/3 cup golden raisins
1/4 teaspoon vanilla
1/2 cup whips cream

Remove crusts from bread. Cover bread slices with paper towels and let stand overnight. Custard: in a heavy medium saucepan combine three egg yolks, light cream, sugar and salt. Cook and stir over medium heat. Continue cooking until mixture coats a metal spoon. Remove from heat; cool at once by setting saucepan in a sink of ice water and stirring for 1-2 minutes. Stir in 1 1/2 teaspoons vanilla. Cover surface with clear plastic wrap. In small bowl combine raisins. Place cherries in another bowl. Heat 3/4 cup sherry till warm. Pour 2/3 cup sherry over cherries. Set aside. Cut bread into 1/2-inch cubes (about 9 cups). In a bowl, fold bread into custard, until coated. Grease a 6 1/2 cup tower mold (without tube). Drain raisins and cherries, reserving sherry. Arrange 1/4 of cherries in bottom of the mold, sprinkle 1/3 cup raisins into the mold. Add 1/4 of bread cube mixture. Sprinkle with 2 tablespoons reserved sherry. Repeat layers three times, arranging cherries and raisins near edges of the mold. Lightly press last layer with back of spoon. Pour remaining reserved sherry over all. Cover mold tightly with foil. Set mold in cooker - for a 5-6qt cooker, pour 1 1/2 cups water around mold (for 3 1/2 -4 qt cooker use 1 cup water). Cover, cook on low 5 1/2 hours or until pudding springs back when touched. Meanwhile make the sherry sauce: in a mixing bowl combine 2 egg yolks, powdered sugar, tablespoons sherry and 1/4 teaspoons vanilla. In small bowl, beat whipping cream until small peaks form. Gently fold whip cream into egg yolk mixture. Cover and chill until serving time. Remove mold from cooker, let stand 10 minutes. Carefully unmold to serving platter. Serve warm with sherry sauce. Serves 12.

Chunk Style Applesauce

8 to 10 large cooking apples, peeled, cored, and sliced or cut in chunks
1/2 cup water
1 tsp cinnamon
1/2 to 1 cup sugar

Put ingredients in crock-pot. Cover; cook on low 8 to 10 hours. Serve warm. add cream if desired.

Cinnamon Apple Bread Pudding

2 tablespoons butter
2 apples, cored peeled, and chopped
3/4 cup brown sugar, divided
1 1/2 teaspoons cinnamon, divided
2 large eggs
12 oz can evaporated milk
3/4 cup apple juice
2 1/2 cups French bread torn in 1/2 to 1- inch pieces

Melt butter in bottom of a 1 1/2 to 2- quart casserole or soufflé dish which will fit in the crock pot. Sprinkle with 2 tablespoons brown sugar and 1/2 teaspoon cinnamon. Add apples. Whisk eggs, milk, and apple juice together; mix in remainder of brown sugar, 1 teaspoon cinnamon, and the bread pieces. Place a trivet or aluminum foil ring in the crock pot. Pour 3/4 cup hot water into the crock pot. Place the casserole dish on the ring in the crock pot. Cover and cook on high for 2 1/2 hours, until knife inserted comes out clean. Serve warm with vanilla ice cream or sweetened whipped cream.

Citrus Fish

1 1/2 lb. fish fillets
Salt and pepper to taste
1 med. onion, chopped
5 tbsp. chopped parsley
4 tsp. oil
2 tsp. grated lemon rind
2 tsp. grated orange rind
Orange and lemon slices

Butter crock pot and put salt and pepper on fish to taste. Then place fish in pot. Put onion, parsley and grated rinds and oil over fish. Cover and cook on low for 1 1/2 hours. Serve garnished with orange and lemon slices.

Clam Chowder

1 can cream of celery soup
1 can cream of mushroom soup
2 cans cream of potato soup
2 cans Campbell's cream of potato soup

1 pt. half and half
3 cans minced clams
Med. onion, precooked in 1/4 c. butter

Mix above ingredients in crock pot and cook on low for 5 hours.

Classic Swiss Fondue

1 clove garlic
2 1/2 cups dry white Rhine, Chablis or Riesling wine
1 tbs lemon juice
1 lb. Swiss cheese, grated
1/2 lb. cheddar cheese, grated
3 tbs flour
3 tbs kirsch
Freshly ground nutmeg
Pepper
Paprika
1 loaf Italian or French bread, cut into 1-inch cubes

Rub an enameled or stainless steel pan with garlic clove. Heat wine to a slow simmer (just under boiling). Add lemon juice. Combine cheeses and flour and gradually stir in. using a figure-8 motion, stir constantly until cheese is melted. Pour into lightly greased crock-pot. Add kirsch; stir well. Sprinkle with nutmeg, pepper and paprika. Cover and cook on high setting for 30 minutes, then turn to low setting for 2 to 5 hours. Keep on low setting while serving. Using fondue forks, dip bread cubes into fondue.
About 2 quarts

Cocktail Kielbasa

2 rings of kielbasa (about 2 lbs)
1 (18 oz) jar apple jelly
1 (9 oz) jar prepared mustard

Slice kielbasa 1/4 to 1/2 inch thick. Mix jelly and mustard in crock pot. Add sliced kielbasa and mix until meat is covered. Set crock pot on low to cook for 2 hours and keep on low while serving. Stir periodically.

Congressional Bean Soup In A Crockpot

1 lb small white beans
8 c water
2 c ham, diced

1 c onion, diced
1 c celery, chopped
2 tab parsley, chopped
1 ts salt
1/4 ts pepper
1 bay leaf

Assemble ingredients in crock pot. Cover and cook on low 8-10 hours or until beans are tender.

Corn Chowder

2 cans (16 oz) whole kernel corn, drained
2 to 3 medium potatoes, chopped
1 onion, chopped
1/2 teaspoon salt
Pepper to taste
2 cups chicken broth
2 cups milk
1/4 cup butter or margarine

Combine first 6 ingredients in crock pot. Cover and cook on low for 7 to 9 hours. Puree in a blender or food processor, if desired, and then return to pot. Stir in milk and butter; cook on high about 1 hour more. Serves 6 to 8.

Country Apples

4-5 cups apples
2 tbsp flour
1/3 cup sugar
1/3 cup raisins
1/4 tsp cinnamon
2/3 cup oatmeal
3 tbsp butter
3/4 cup brown sugar

Peel, slice and coat apples with flour and 1/3 cup sugar. Stir in the raisins, cinnamon, and oatmeal. Pour 1 cup water into crockery. Add apple mix. Pour melted butter over apples and then brown sugar. Cook on low 4-6 hours. Serves 6.

Country Captain Chicken Breasts

2 medium-size granny smith apples
1 small onion, finely chopped
1 small green bell pepper, seeded and finely chopped
3 cloves garlic, minced or pressed
2 tablespoons dried currants
1 tablespoon curry powder
1 teaspoon ground ginger
1/4 teaspoon ground red pepper (cayenne)
1 can (about 14 1/2 oz.) diced tomatoes
6 small skinless, boneless chicken breast halves (about 1 3/4 lbs. total)
1/2 cup chicken broth
1 cup long-grain white rice
1 pound large raw shrimp, shelled and deveined
1/3 cup slivered almonds
Salt
Chopped parsley

Quarter, core, and dice unpeeled apples. in a 4-quart or larger electric crock pot, combine apples, onion, bell pepper, garlic, currants, curry powder, ginger, and red pepper; stir in tomatoes. Rinse chicken and pat dry; then arrange, overlapping pieces slightly, on top of tomato mixture. Pour in broth. Cover and cook at low setting until chicken is very tender when pierced (6 to 7 hours). Carefully lift chicken to a warm plate, cover lightly, and keep warm in a 200 degree oven. Stir rice into cooking liquid. Increase cooker heat setting to high; cover and cook, stirring once or twice, until rice is almost tender to bite (30 to 35 minutes). Stir in shrimp, cover and cook until shrimp are opaque in center; cut to test (about 10 more minutes). Meanwhile, toast almonds in a small nonstick frying pan over medium heat until golden brown (5 to 8 minutes), stirring occasionally. Set aside. To serve, season rice mixture to taste with salt. Mound in a warm serving dish; arrange chicken on top. Sprinkle with parsley and almonds. Makes 6 servings.

Crab Dip

1 lb. Velveeta cheese
1 lb. butter or margarine
2 cans crab meat
Heat together. Keep warm in fondue or crock pot. Serve with bread sticks.

Cranberry Apple Turkey Breast

2 teaspoons melted butter or margarine
1/2 cup chicken broth
1 large apple, cored and chopped
1/2 cup chopped onion
1 stalk celery, chopped
1 cup whole berry cranberry sauce
3/4 teaspoon poultry seasoning
2 cups seasoned crumb-style stuffing
2 to 3 pounds turkey breast cutlets.

Combine butter, chicken broth, apple, onion, celery, cranberry sauce, poultry seasoning and stuffing. Place 3 tablespoons stuffing mix on each turkey cutlet. Roll up and tie. Place in stoneware. Cover; cook on low 8 hours (high 4 hours).

Cranberry Cocktail Meatballs

2 pounds ground beef
1 cup cornflake crumbs
2 eggs
1/2 cup chopped, fresh parsley
1/3 cup ketchup
3 tablespoons minced onions
2 tablespoons soy sauce
1/4 teaspoon garlic powder
1/4 teaspoon pepper sauce
16 ounces can jelly or whole cranberry sauce
12 ounces chili sauce
1 tablespoon brown sugar
1 tablespoon lemon juice

In a large bowl, combine ground beef, cornflake crumbs, parsley, eggs, ketchup, onion, soy sauce, garlic powder and pepper. Mix well and form into small balls, from 1/2" to 3/4" in diameter. Place in a casserole or baking pan. Heat oven to 300 degrees f. meanwhile in a saucepan, combine cranberry sauce, chili sauce, brown sugar and lemon juice. Cook stirring over medium heat until smooth. Pour hot sauce over meatballs in casserole. Bake for 30 to 45 minutes, depending on the size of the meatballs. Transfer to crock pot and keep on low for serving.

Cream Cheese Crockpot Chicken

1 frying chicken, cut up
2 tbsp melted butter
Salt and pepper to taste
1 package of dry Italian seasoning mix
1 can cream of chicken soup
1 8 oz brick of cream cheese, cut up in cubes
1/2 c chicken broth
1 large onion crushed garlic to taste

Brush chicken with butter and sprinkle with the dry Italian seasoning mix. Cover and cook on low for 6-7 hours. About 45 minutes before done, brown the onion in the butter and then add the cream cheese, soup, and chicken broth to the saucepan. Add the crushed garlic and stir all ingredients until smooth. Add salt and pepper to taste. Pour sauce mixture over chicken in crock pot and cook an additional 30-45 minutes. Remove chicken to platter and stir sauce before putting in gravy.

Creamy Chicken And Rice

Chicken tenders (3 per person)
Cream of mushroom soup (1 can for 2-3 people, 2 for 4-6)
Mrs. Grass onion soup mix (1 per each can of soup)
1 tbsp olive oil
Long grain brown rice (1 cup per can of soup)
1 tbsp whole thyme, crushed
Salt and pepper to taste
desired amount of broccoli florettes (optional)
diced red pepper (optional)

When using brown rice, you need 2 1/4 cups liquid for each 1 cup rice. Empty can of soup into a measuring cup, and add water (or white wine) to equal 2 ½. Heat olive oil in a sauté pan, and add rice until it begins to crackle, but not brown. Whisk together the soups and additional h2o, herbs and seasonings. Combine all ingredients (except veggies) in Crockpot, and cook on high 4-6 hours, or 8-10 hours on low. During last 30-45 minutes, add desired veggies.

Creamy Corn

2 cups corn
2 tablespoons sugar
2 eggs
1/4 cup flour

2 tablespoons butter
1 cup milk
1/2 teaspoon salt

Mix corn, sugar, eggs, flour, butter, milk and salt; place in crock pot. Cook on high for one hour.

Creamy Orange Cheesecake

Crust:
3/4 cup cookie or graham cracker crumbs
2 tablespoons sugar
3 tablespoons melted butter

Filling: 16 ounces cream cheese (light)
2/3 cup sugar
2 eggs
1 egg yolk
1/4 cup frozen orange juice concentrate, thawed
1 teaspoon orange or lemon zest or dried grated rind
1 tablespoon flour
1/2 teaspoon vanilla

Combine crumbs with sugar; mix in melted butter until well moistened. Pat into a 7-inch spring form pan. In a medium bowl, cream together the cream cheese and sugar. Add eggs and yolk and beat for about 3 minutes on medium with a hand-held electric mixer. Beat in orange juice, zest, flour, and vanilla. Beat for another 2 minutes. Pour batter into prepared crust; place on a rack or aluminum foil ring in the crockery cooker. Cover and cook on high for 2 1/2 to 3 hours. Turn off and leave for 1 to 2 hours, until cool enough to remove. Cool completely and remove the sides of the pan. Chill before serving, and store leftovers in the refrigerator.

Creamy Scalloped Potatoes

3 cups thinly sliced carrots
3 tablespoons butter or margarine
2 cups water
3 tablespoons orange marmalade
1/4 teaspoon salt
2 tablespoons chopped pecans

Combine carrots, water, and salt in crock pot. Cover and cook on high 2 to 3 hours or until the carrots are done. Drain well; stir in remaining ingredients. Cover and cook on high 20-30 minutes. Makes 5 to 6 servings.

Creamy Spinach Dip

8 ounces cream cheese, cubed
5 ounces frozen chopped spinach
2 tablespoons pimento, diced
1 teaspoon Worcestershire sauce
1/4 teaspoon garlic salt
1/4 cup whips cream
2 tablespoons parmesan cheese, grated
2 teaspoons onion, finely chopped
1/2 teaspoon thyme

Combine cream cheese and cream in crock pot. Cover and heat until cheese is melted, 30 to 60 minutes. Add remaining ingredients. Cover and heat 30 minutes. Serve with raw vegetables, crackers, or bread pieces.

Crocked Kielbasa

1/2 pound lean ground beef
1 pound kielbasa sausage -- sliced
1 can whole tomatoes -- (28 ounces) undrained
9 ounces frozen French-cut green beans
1 can pitted black olives -- (6 ounces) (drained and left whole)
1/2 cup red wine
3 garlic cloves -- minced
1 medium onion -- sliced
1 medium green pepper -- chopped
1 teaspoon basil -- crushed
1 teaspoon oregano -- crushed
1/2 teaspoon thyme -- crushed
1/4 teaspoon pepper
1 pound pasta of your choice
4 ounces parmesan -- freshly grated

In a medium skillet, sauté ground beef. When browned, transfer to Crockpot. Add all other ingredients except pasta and parmesan simmer on low for 6-8 hours. Cook pasta according to. Ladle crocked kielbasa over pasta in large bowls. Pass the parmesan cheese to garnish.

Crockpot Almost Lasagna

1 box retina (or ziti), any fun, flavorful pasta will do
2 - 28-oz jars pasta sauce (one with tomato chunks works well)
1 egg
1/2 lb ground beef
1/2 lb sausage
2 tbsp olive oil
1 c. parmesan cheese
1/2 c Italian breadcrumbs
1 bag mozzarella cheese
16-20 oz. ricotta cheese
2 eggs
1 c. parmesan cheese
1 1/2 tsp. parsley flakes dash
Salt & pepper

Grease crock-pot, or spray with non-stick cooking spray. Cook rotini according to package, drain. Brown and drain meat. Toss pasta with olive oil. Add pasta sauce to mixture, toss well. Stir together parmesan cheese, breadcrumbs, egg, 1/2 bag mozzarella cheese, and browned meat. Can sprinkle lightly with garlic powder. Beat together ricotta, 2 eggs, parmesan, parsley, salt & pepper. Pour half of pasta/sauce/meat mixture into crock-pot. Spread entire ricotta mixture over first layer of pasta. Cover ricotta layer with remaining pasta mixture, and cover with remaining cheese. Cover, and cook on low 4-6 hours.

Crockpot Apple And Brown Sugar Corned Beef

1 corned beef brisket
1 quart apple juice
1 cup brown sugar
1 tbsp prepared mustard
8 small red potatoes
2 medium carrots, pared and cut into chunks
1 onion, peeled and cut into eights
1/2 head cabbage, cut into chunks

Place all ingredients in large crock pot (cut meat in half if necessary). Stir to mix. Cook on high for 4 to 5 hours on high or 8 to 10 hours on low. Remove meat and vegetables and some of the cooking liquid. Slice meat thinly across the grain. Serve with the vegetables and some of the liquid.

Crockpot Apple Brown Betty

3 lbs. cooking apples
10 slices of bread, cubed (about 4 cups)
1/2 tsp. cinnamon
1/4 tsp. nutmeg
1/8 tsp. salt
3/4 c. brown sugar
1/2 c. butter or margarine, melted

Wash apples, peel, core, cut into eighths; place in bottom on crock. Combine bread cubes, cinnamon, nutmeg, salt, sugar, butter; toss together. Place on top of apples in crock. Cover. Place crock into outer shell. Cook on low setting 2 to 4 hours. Makes 6 to 8 servings.

Crockpot Apple Butter I

Apples -- cut up, to fill 3 1/2 qt. Crockpot
1 cup brown sugar
1 cup apple cider
Juice of 1 lemon
1 tablespoon cinnamon

Cut blemishes off apples and cut into chunks to fill 3 1/2 qt. Crockpot. Add sugar, cider and lemon juice. Cover and cook on low for 8 hours. Stir. Add cinnamon and cook another 10 hours. Stir occasionally until brown. Run through food mill or any strainer to strain out seeds and skins. To thicken, if not thick enough, return to crock pot and cook on high uncovered until desired consistency. Makes 3-4 pints.

Crockpot Apple Butter II

Peel and core apples, cut in quarters, enough to fill a 4 quart Crockpot to about 1 1/2 inches from the top:

Add:
4 tsp. cinnamon
1/2 tsp cloves
1/2 tsp salt
3 cups sugar

Start on high with about 4 tb water, till it gets hot, then turn on low and cook all day. When it is done and apples are fully cooked down put small amounts into food processor and zap quickly till smooth.

Crockpot Apple Butter III

4 lbs apples, cored and sliced (don't peel)
1 1/3 cups packed brown sugar
1 cup apple cider
Grated zest and juice of one lemon
3 tbs grated ginger

Combine apples, brown sugar, apple cider, zest, juice. Cover and cook 8-10 hours on low, till apples are very soft. Then stir in ginger, increase heat to high, uncover and cook (stirring now and then) till mixture is reduced to about 3 cups for 8 to 10 hours. Put the resulting mash through a food mill.

Crockpot Apple Butter IV

2 qt. sweet cider
4lbs apples, peeled, cored & sliced
3 c. sugar
1/4 tsp. cinnamon
1/4 tsp. allspice
1/8 tsp. cloves
1 tsp. salt
Place apples & cider in crock pot. Cover & cook on low 10 - 12 hrs. Do not stir!!!!!!! Put apples through a fine mesh strainer. Mash apples. Add equal parts sugar stirring well between each; add spices & salt stir well!! Return to crock-pot. cook on high 1 hr. pour into 1/2 pint jars, seal and process 10 min. makes 5 half pints.

Crockpot Apple Cake Dessert

6 apples peeled, cored and sliced
Sugar
Cinnamon
8 oz of yellow cake mix
1/4 c melted butter or margarine

Put slices of apples in crock pot. Pour half a package of dry cake mix over apples. Drizzle butter over cake mix. Sprinkle cinnamon and sugar mixture over that and cook on low 1 1/2 to 2 hours. Keep checking and it's done when the apples are soft.

Crockpot Apple Caramel Dessert

2 med apples
1/2 c apple juice
7 oz caramel candy
1 tsp vanilla
1/8 tsp ground cardamom
1/2 tsp ground cinnamon
1/3 c peanut butter, creamy
7 slices angel food cake
1 qt vanilla ice cream

Peel, core and cut each apple into 18 wedges; set aside. Combine apple juice, unwrapped caramel candies, vanilla, cardamom and cinnamon. Drop peanut butter, 1 tsp at a time, over ingredients in crock pot and stir. Add apple wedges; cover and cook on low for 5 hrs. Stir thoroughly, and then cook 1 hr more. Serve approx 1/3 cup of warm mixture over a slice of angel food cake or ice cream.

Crockpot Apple Cider

1 gallon of apple cider

Put it in a crock pot. Add 3 cinnamon sticks, about a tsp of whole cloves, and about 3 or 4 whole allspice. Slice up an orange and put orange rings in there. Put it on low and let it simmer all day. Remove the spices and oranges when the flavor reaches the taste you prefer.

Crockpot Apple Coconut Crisps

4 large granny smith apples, peeled & coarsely sliced (about 4 cups)
1/2 cup sweetened flaked coconut
1 tablespoon flour
1/3 cup brown sugar
1/2 cup butterscotch or caramel ice cream topping
1/2 teaspoon cinnamon
1/3 cup flour
1/2 cup quick rolled oats
2 tablespoons butter or margarine

In a casserole 1 1/2-quart baking dish that fits in the Crockpot, combine apples with coconut, 1 tablespoon flour, 1/3 cup brown sugar, and cinnamon. Drizzle with the ice cream topping. Combine remaining ingredients in a small bowl with a fork or pastry cutter and sprinkle over apple mixture. Cover and cook on high for 2 1/2 to3 hours, until apples are tender. Serve warm with vanilla ice cream or whipped topping.

Crockpot Apple Dessert I

6 apples, peeled and sliced
2/3 cup raw oatmeal
2/3 cup sugar
1/3 cup flour
1 tsp cinnamon
1/4 tsp nutmeg
1/4 tsp ginger
1/3 cup butter or margarine, melted

Mix oatmeal, sugar, flour, and spices in small bowl. Stir melted butter into mixture until it is crumbly. Put about half of sliced apples in Crockpot and spoon about half of oatmeal mixture on top. Cover with the rest of the apples and top with the rest of the crumbly mixture. Cook on high about 2 1/2 hours.

Crockpot Apple Dessert II

2 cups milk
1/4 cup brown sugar
1 tbsp melted butter
1/4 tsp salt
1/2 tsp cinnamon
1 cup rolled oats, regular
1 cup chopped apples
1/2 cup raisons

Spray or butter inside of crock pot. Add ingredients to pot and stir cover and cook on low overnight.

Crockpot Apple Pie

8 tart apples peeled and sliced
1 1/4 t ground cinnamon
1/4 t allspice
1/4 t nutmeg
3/4 cup milk
2 t butter soften
3/4 c sugar
2 eggs
1 t vanilla
1/2 c bisquick
1 c bisquick

1/3 c brown sugar

3 t cold butter

Toss apples in large bowl with cinnamon, allspice, and nutmeg. Place in lightly greased Crockpot. Combine milk, softened butter, sugar, eggs, vanilla, and the 1/2 c bisquick. Spoon over apples. Combine the 1 cup bisquick and brown sugar. Cut the cold butter into mixture until crumbly. Sprinkle this mixture over top of apple mixture. Cover and cook on low 6-7 hours or until apples are soft.

Crockpot Apple Sauce

About 3 pounds apples, peeled, cored, and sliced

1/3 cup sugar

1 cinnamon stick

2 tbs lemon juice

Nutmeg

Put apples in cooker, sprinkle w/sugar and add cinnamon stick. Sprinkle lemon juice on. Cover and cook on low for 6 1/2 to 8 hours till apples form a thick sauce. Sprinkle with nutmeg to taste.

Crockpot Arroz Con Pollo

4 chicken breast halves, skin and excess fat removed

1/4 teaspoon salt

1/4 teaspoon pepper

1/4 teaspoon paprika

1 tablespoon oil

1 medium onion, chopped

1 small red pepper, chopped

1 clove of garlic, minced

1/2 teaspoon dried rosemary leaves

1 14 1/2 ounce can crushed tomatoes

1 10 oz package frozen peas

Season chicken with salt, pepper, and paprika. In a medium skillet, heat oil over medium-high heat. Add chicken and brown. Put chicken in the crock-pot. In a small bowl, combine remaining ingredients except the peas. Pour over chicken. Cover: cook on low 7-9 hours (high 3-4 hours) one hour before serving, add peas. Serve over rice. Makes 4 servings.

Crockpot Artichoke, Chicken And Olives

1 1/2 lbs skinless, boneless chicken breast halves and/or thighs
2 c sliced fresh mushrooms
1 (14.5 oz) can diced tomatoes
1 (8 or 9 oz) pkg frozen artichokes
1 c chicken broth
1 med onion, chopped
1/2 c sliced pitted ripe olives (or 1/4 cup capers, drained)
1/4 c dry white wine or chicken broth
3 tbsp quick cooking tapioca
2-3 tsp curry powder
3/4 tsp dried thyme, crushed
1/4 tsp salt
1/4 tsp pepper
4 c hot cooked couscous

Rinse chicken & set aside. in a 3 1/2 qt crock pot combine mushrooms, undrained tomatoes, frozen artichoke hearts, chicken broth, onion, olives, & wine/broth. Stir in tapioca, curry powder, thyme, salt, & pepper. Add chicken. Spoon some of the tomato mixture over chicken. Cover & cook on low for 7 to 8 hours or on high for 3 1/2 to 4 hours. Serve with hot cooked couscous. Serves 6.

Crockpot Artichokes

5 artichokes, remove stalks and tough leaves
1 1/2 tsp salt
8 peppercorns
2 stalks celery, cut up
1/2 lemon, sliced
2 c boiling water

Combine all ingredients in Crockpot. Cook on high 4 - 5 hours.

Crockpot Autumn Chicken

2 large or 4 small chicken breasts
2 parsnips
2 carrots
1 acorn squash
1 14.5 oz. can of chicken broth
Garlic salt
Pepper

Nutmeg
Honey

Peel and chop carrots and parsnips and place them in the bottom of the Crockpot. Sprinkle with garlic. Place chicken on top. Pour in broth. Cut squash into chunks and slice off the skin. Place on top of chicken. Sprinkle desired amounts of salt, pepper and nutmeg on top of squash and drizzle enough honey on top to lightly cover the squash. Cook on low 8-10 hours.

Crockpot Autumn Pork Chops

6 pork chops
2 medium acorn squash -- unpeeled
3/4 teaspoon salt
2 tablespoons melted butter
3/4 cup brown sugar -- packed
3/4 teaspoon brown bouquet sauce
1 tablespoon orange juice
1/2 teaspoon orange peel -- grated

Trim excess fat from chops. Cut each squash into 4 to 5 crosswise slices; remove seeds. Arrange 3 chops on bottom of slow-cooking pot. Place all squash slices on top; then another layer of remaining 3 chops. Combine salt, butter, sugar, bouquet sauce, orange juice, and orange peel. Spoon over chops. Cover and cook on low for 4 to 6 hours or until done. Serve one or two slices of squash with each pork chop.

Crockpot Autumn Pork Roast

3 to 4 lb. pork roast
Salt & pepper
1 c. cranberries, finely chopped
1/4 c. honey
1 tsp. grated orange peel
1/8 tsp. ground cloves
1/8 tsp. ground nutmeg

Sprinkle roast with salt and pepper. Place in slow cooking Crockpot. Combine remaining ingredients. Pour over roast. Cover. Cook on low for 8 to 10 hours. Or on high for 4-5 .makes 6 to 8 servings.

Crockpot Aztec Black Beans

1 lb. dried black beans
16 oz. jar of salsa

Rinse black beans, removing any stones or foreign objects. Cover with water, soak all night. Drain beans and place in crock pot with salsa. Add enough water to just cover beans. Cover and cook on low 8-10 hours.

Crockpot Baked Apples

2 tbsp raisins
1/4 cup sugar
6 to 8 apples, washed and cored
1 tsp cinnamon
2 tbsp butter

Mix raisins and sugar, fill center of apples. Sprinkle with cinnamon and dot with butter. Put in Crockpot; add 1/2 cup water. Cover; cook on low 7 to 9 hours.

Crockpot Baked Beans I

1 pound dried small white beans -- rinsed
4 1/2 cups water
1/3 cup molasses
1/4 cup brown sugar
1 onion -- chopped
1/4 pound salt pork -- cut into 1" cubes
1 tablespoon Dijon-style mustard
1/2 teaspoon salt

In slow-cooker, combine all ingredients. Cover and cook on low 13 to 14 hours, stirring occasionally, if possible.

Crockpot Baked Beans II

1 lb ground beef
3/4 lb bacon fried and diced
1 onion lg chopped and browned
1 lg can pork and beans
1 16 oz kidney beans canned
1 16 oz buttered Lima beans canned
1 cup catsup 3 tbsp white vinegar

1/4 cup liquid smoke
1 tsp salt dash pepper

Put all ingredients in crock pot cook 4-6 hrs on low. The longer you cook it the better it will taste.

Crockpot Baked Beans III

2 cans cannellini beans
2 cans black beans
2 cans red kidney beans
1 cans chick peas
2 diced onions
2 tablespoons mustard
1 cup molasses
1/2 cup brown sugar
3/4 cup maple syrup
Rinse and drain beans and set aside.

On bottom of Crockpot place diced onions, and then dump on beans. Then drizzle on all other ingredients. Don't stir. It will look dry for awhile. Crock pot on high for 6-8 hours

Crockpot Baked Beans IV

24 to 32 oz. canned pork and beans, undrained
3/4 cup firmly packed brown sugar
1 cup ketchup
1 large onion, diced
1 tsp. prepared mustard
2 to 3 slices bacon

Combine all ingredients in crock pot. Cover and cook on low about 6 hours.

Crockpot Barbecued Short Ribs

2 c. water
3 or 4 lbs. boneless short ribs
18 oz. bottle barbecue sauce
1 tbsp. Worcestershire sauce
3 oz. Heinz 57 hickory smoke sauce
1/4 tsp. angostura
1/4 tbsp. lemon pepper seasoning

Combine water, barbecue sauce, Worcestershire, Heinz 57 sauce, angostura, lemon pepper and short ribs in crock pot on low heat for 12 hours.

Crockpot Beans

1 lb. ground beef
3/4 lb. fried crumbled bacon
1 c. chopped onions
1 c. ketchup
1/4 c. brown sugar
1/2 tsp. pepper
1 tsp. hickory smoke flavoring
1 lb. cans each pork and beans, lima beans, butter beans, and kidney beans

Cook on low in Crockpot for 4-8 hours. The longer it cooks, the smokier it tastes.

Crockpot Beef And Beans

1 1/2 lbs of stewing beef
1 tbsp. prepared mustard
1 tbsp. taco seasoning
1/2 tsp. salt
1/4 tsp. pepper
2 garlic cloves minced
1 can 16 oz diced tomatoes, undrained
1 med. onion chopped
1 can kidney beans rinsed and drained
1 cans chili beans

Combine mustard, taco seasonings, salt, pepper and garlic in a large bowl. Add beef and toss to coat! Put the beef in your crock pot and add the rest of the ingredients. Cover and cook for 6 -8 hours on low. Serve over hot rice!

Crockpot Beef And Chipotle Burritos

1 1/2 lb. boneless beef round steak, cut 3/4" thick
1 14 1 /2 oz. can dice tomatoes
1 sm. onion, chopped
1 to 2 canned chipotle peppers in adobo sauce, chopped
1 tsp. dried oregano, crushed
1/4 tsp. ground cumin
1 clove garlic, minced
6 9-10" tomato-flavored or plain flour tortillas, warmed

3/4 c. shredded sharp cheddar cheese (3 oz.)
1 recipe pico de gallo salsa
Shredded jicama or radishes
Dairy sour cream (optional)

Trim fat from meat. Cut meat into 6 pieces. in a 3 1/2 or 4 qt. crockery cooker place meat, undrained tomatoes, onion, peppers, oregano, cumin, and garlic. Cover; cook on low-heat setting for 8 to 10 hours or on high-heat setting for 4 to 5 hours. Remove meat from cooker. Using 2 forks, shred meat. Spoon one-sixth of the meat onto each warm tortilla just below the center. Top with cheese, pico de gallo salsa, and if desired, jicama or radishes and sour cream. Roll up tortilla. Makes 6 servings

Pico de gallo salsa: combine 2 medium finely chopped tomatoes; 2 tbsp. finely chopped onion; 2 tbsp. snipped cilantro; 1 Serrano pepper; finely chopped; and dash sugar. Cover; chill several hours.

Crockpot Beef And Gravy

2-3 pounds roast cut into bite sized pieces
1 packet Lipton's onion soup mix
2 cans cream of mushroom soup

Place pieces of roast in crock pot. Sprinkle packet of onion soup on meat. Cover with cream of mushroom soup. Let cook up to 9 hours. Stir about 1/2 way through cooking.

Crockpot Beef Bourguignon I

1 cup dry red wine
2 tablespoons olive oil
1 large onion -- sliced
1/2 teaspoon thyme
2 tablespoons parsley -- chopped
1 bay leaf
1/4 teaspoon pepper
2 pounds stewing beef, cut into 1 1/2-inch cubes
3 slices bacon (thick-cut is possible) -- diced
12 small white onions
1/2 pound sliced mushrooms
2 cloves garlic -- minced
1 teaspoon salt

Combine first seven ingredients, mix well, add beef. Marinate at least 3 hours (overnight if refrigerated) drain meat, reserving marinade. In skillet, sauté bacon and remove. Brown meat in bacon fat. Combine beef, bacon, vegetables and seasonings in crock pot. Pour over enough marinade to cover. Cook on low 8-10 hours.

Crockpot Beef Bourguignon II

1 lb. bacon, cooked, reserve grease
3 lbs. beef, cubed
1 bottle red wine
1 lb. onion, chopped
1 lb. celery
1 lb. carrots, chopped
2 cloves garlic, chopped
Chopped shallots (optional)
1 bay leaf salt & pepper

Flour slowly cook bacon in large baking pan; remove. Dredge beef cubes in flour, brown in bacon fat. Transfer meat from skillet to heated platter. sauté vegetable and garlic in bacon fat; remove. Drain fat from pan. Gently combine beef, vegetables, bacon and half the wine. Add bay leaf and salt and pepper to taste. Cook on low 8 - 10 hours.

Crockpot Beef Burger Stroganoff

1 1/2 lbs lean ground beef
3 slices bacon, diced
1 small onion, chopped
2 tbs flour
1/4 tsp paprika
1 tsp salt
1 can (10 3/4oz) condensed cream of mushroom soup
2 tbs dry red wine
1 cup dairy sour cream
6 to 8 hamburger buns, toasted and buttered

In large skillet, brown beef and bacon until red color disappears. Drain. In Crockpot, mix together drained beef, bacon, onion, flour, paprika, and salt. Stir in undiluted soup and wine. Cover pot and cook on low 4 to 5 hours. Stir in sour cream. Spoon mixture over toasted buns. Serves 6 to 8.

Crockpot Beef Burgundy I

2 slices bacon -- chopped
2 pounds sirloin tip or round steak -- cut in 1 inch cubes
1/4 cup flour
1 teaspoon salt
1/2 teaspoon seasoned salt
1/4 teaspoon marjoram
1/4 teaspoon thyme
1/4 teaspoon pepper
1 clove garlic -- minced
1 cube beef bouillon -- crushed
1 cup burgundy wine
2 tablespoons cornstarch

In large skillet cook bacon several minutes. Remove bacon and set aside. Coat beef with flour and brown on all sides in bacon mixture. Combine steak, bacon drippings, cooked bacon, seasonings, bouillon and burgundy in crock pot. Cover and cook on low for 6 to 8 hours or until meat is tender. Turn control to high. Add cornstarch (dissolved in 2 tablespoons water); cook on high 15 minutes. Serves 6.

Crockpot Beef Burgundy II

3 lbs beef, cut in large cubes-can use stew beef or round steak
1 cans minestrone soup
1 cans tomato bisque soup
1 can cream of mushroom soup
1 envelope dry onion soup mix
1 soup cans burgundy wine

Flour and brown meat. Place in Crockpot. Mix remaining ingredients and pour over meat. Cook on low 6-8 hours. Serve over noodles or rice. You could cook the rice at home and reheat in the micro at work.

Crockpot Beef Fajitas

1 1/2 pounds beef flank steak
1 cup chopped onion
1 green sweet pepper, cut into 1/2 inch pieces
1 jalapeno pepper, chopped
1 tbsp. cilantro
2 garlic cloves, minced (or 1/4 tsp. garlic powder)
1 tsp. chili powder

1 tsp. ground cumin

1 tsp. ground coriander

1/2 tsp. salt

1 can (8oz) chopped tomatoes

12 8inch flour tortillas

Toppings: sour cream, guacamole, shredded cheddar cheese and salsa

Cut flank steak into 6 portions. In any size Crockpot combine meat, onion, green pepper, jalapeno pepper, cilantro, garlic, chili powder, cumin, coriander and salt. Add tomatoes. Cover and cook on low 8-10 hours or high 4-5 hours. Remove meat from Crockpot and shred. Return meat to Crockpot and stir. To serve, spread meat mixture into flour tortillas and top with toppings. Roll up.

Crockpot Beef For Sandwiches

1 roast

1 packet Italian dressing mix or ranch dressing mix or 2 packages onion soup mix

1 cup water

Place all in Crockpot, cook on low 8 hours.

Crockpot Beef N Brew Vegetable Soup

3 medium onions, sliced

1 lb carrots cut into 1/2" slices

4 parsnips cut into 1/2" slices

2 bay leaves

4 cloves garlic, minced

1 tbs snipped fresh thyme or 1 tsp dried thyme, crushed

1/2 tsp pepper

2 tbs quick cooking tapioca

1 1/2 lbs beef stew meat, cut into 1" cubes

1 14 1/2 oz can beef broth

1 12 oz can beer

in a 5 or 6 quart Crockpot, place onions, carrots, parsnips, garlic, bay leaves, dried thyme, and pepper. Sprinkle with tapioca. Place meat on top of vegetables. Add beef broth and beer. Cover; cook on low-heat setting for 10 to 12 hours or on high-heat setting for 5 to 6 hours. To serve, remove bay leaves; if using fresh thyme, stir in now.

Crockpot Beef Pot Roast

1 1/2 lb- 2lb. pot roast meat
1 dry package of good season's garlic dressing
1 dry pkg of Italian (or zesty Italian) dressing
1 can of beer (your choice-not dark)

Place one envelope of good seasons in bottom of crock pot. Place meat on top, top with other package of dressing and pour beer over all. Let cook 8-10 hours on low.

Crockpot Beef Stew I

2 lbs. stew beef
1/4 c. flour
1 tsp. paprika
4 lg. carrots
3 lg. potatoes
1 c. condensed beef broth
1 1/2 tsp. salt
1/2 tsp. pepper
1/3 c. soy sauce
1 lg. onion
1 cans tomato sauce (8 oz.)

Layer potatoes, then carrots. Top with meat; sprinkle meat with soy sauce, salt, paprika, pepper & flour. Spread with chopped onions. Combine beef broth & tomato sauce & pour overall. Cover
& cook on low 7 - 8 hrs. Or high 4 - 5 hrs.

Crockpot Beef Stew II

1 lb. beef bourguignon (or cheaper cut)
3 large sweet potatoes (cut into 1" thick slices)
2 cans beef bouillon (or broth or consommé)
2 small cans tomato paste
3-4 handfuls of assorted veggies
1 lb. fresh mushrooms (quartered)
1 large onion (diced)
2 cloves garlic (minced)
1/4 cup flour

Mix bite sized pieces of meat in flour, brown in some oil along with the diced garlic. While meat is browning, combine beef bouillon & tomato paste in a crock pot, mix well. Pre-cook the sweet potatoes until just tender, add to crock pot along with onions and any raw veggies that you may use. Add enough water to cover and cook on low for as long as you want.

Crockpot Beef Stew III

1 package stew beef
1 can cream of potato soup
1 can cream of mushroom soup
1 - 1 1/2 cans of water

Cook on high all day (7-8) hours

Crockpot Beef Stroganoff I

2 lbs top round steak, sliced thin across the grain
1 lb fresh mushrooms, sliced
1 medium onion, sliced
1/4 tsp thyme
3/4 cup dry sherry
3/4 cup beef broth (Swanson's)
3/4 tsp dry mustard
1/4 tsp garlic salt

Put all this in the Crockpot, stir well and cook on low for 8 hours. Turn heat to high and mix 1-1/2 cup sour cream 1/2 cup wonder flour, cake flour works too, heat on high for 40 minutes. Serve over rice or noodles.

Crockpot Beef Stroganoff II

1 1/2 lb. lean ground beef
1 medium onion, chopped
1 clove garlic, minced
3 tbsp. tomato paste
1/2 c. beef broth
3 tbsp. sherry
1 tsp. salt
Dash pepper
1 can mushrooms, drained
1 c. sour cream

Brown ground beef with onion and garlic; drain. Add to crock pot with remaining ingredients except for sour cream. Cover and cook on low for 5 to 7 hours. Stir in sour cream. Heat through. Serve over egg noodles.

Crockpot Beef Stroganoff III

3 lb. beef round steak, 1/2 inch thick
1/2 c. flour
2 tsp. salt
1/8 tsp. pepper
1/2 tsp. dry mustard
2 med. onions, thinly sliced and separated into rings
2 (4 oz. each) cans
Sliced mushrooms, drained or 1/2 lb. mushrooms, sliced
1 (10 1/2 oz.) can condensed beef broth
1/4 c. dry white wine (optional)
1 1/2 c. sour cream
1/4 c. flour

Trim all excess fat from steak and cut meat into 3 inch strips about 1/2 inches wide. Combine 1/2 cup flour, the salt, pepper and dry mustard; toss with steak strips to coat thoroughly. Place coated steak strips in crock pot; stir in onion rings and mushrooms. Add beef broth and wine; stir well. Cover and cook on low setting for 8-10 hours. Before serving, combine sour cream with 1/4 cup flour; stir into crock pot. Serve stroganoff over rice or noodles.

Crockpot Beef Stroganoff IV

1 can cream of mushroom soup
1 package onion soup mix
1 package mushroom
1 onion cut in rings
1 package beef stew meat
Salt and pepper

Put in crock pot and cook all day. Add 16 oz sour cream before serving. Serve over egg noodles.

Crockpot Beef Taco Bean Soup

2 lbs. rump roast
1 pkg taco seasoning
1 can Mexican style diced tomatoes (15 oz.)
1 small can green chiles
1 cans tomato sauce (8 oz)
1 onion - chopped
2 beef bouillon cubes

2 cans red kidney beans, (15 oz. each), rinsed, drained
Shredded cheddar cheese

Cut roast into bite sized chunks. Roll in taco seasoning and add to crock pot. Then add the tomatoes, chiles, tomato sauce, onion, and bouillon cubes. Cover and cook on low 6 hours or until meat is tender.
Add the drained beans and cook until the beans are heated through; around 30 minutes. Serve topped with cheese, and/or the toppings that you like.

Crockpot Beef Tips

1/2 c flour
1 tsp salt
1/8 tsp pepper
4 lb beef or sirloin tips
1/2 c chopped green onions
2 c sliced mushrooms (4 oz. can, drained) or 1/2 lb mushrooms, sliced
1 can condensed beef broth, (10 1/2 oz.)
1 tsp Worcestershire sauce
2 tsp tomato paste or ketchup
1/4 c dry red wine or water
3 tbsp flour
1 buttered noodles

Combine 1/2 cup flour with the salt and pepper and toss with beef cubes to coat thoroughly. Place in crock-pot. Add green onions and drained mushrooms. Combine with beef broth, Worcestershire sauce and tomato paste or ketchup. Pour over beef and vegetables; stir well. Cover and cook on low setting for 7 to 12 hours. One hour before serving, turn to high setting. Make a smooth paste of red wine and 3 tablespoons flour; stir into crock-pot, mixing well.

Crockpot Best Pork Roast

4-5 pound pork roast
6-8 cloves garlic
Pepper
Basil
1 c dry white wine
Onion

Cut 6-8 holes into the roast just big enough to fit a clove of garlic. Put a garlic clove (peeled) into each hole. Rub outside with cracked pepper and basil. Pour dry white wine in the bottom of the crock pot. Place roast in the crock pot put slices or wedges of onion on top and around the roast. Cover and cook on low all day or until done.

Crockpot Black Bean Chili

3/4 cup cooked black beans
1 lb. stew beef, cubed
3 tablespoons oil
1/4 cup chopped onion
1/4 cup chopped green peppers
1/2 cup diced green chilies
3 tbsp. tomato paste
3 to 4 beef bouillon cubes, or beef base
1/4 tsp. ground cumin
1 tsp. minced garlic
1/2 tsp. salt and pepper
1 cup shredded Monterey jack or cheddar cheese

Brown stews beef in oil with onion and green pepper. Combine all ingredients except cheese and cook 6 to 8 hours on low. Sprinkle cheese over individual servings.

Crockpot Black Bean Chili With Pork

1 lb. boneless pork, cut into cubes
2 (16 oz.) cans black beans, drained
1 red or yellow bell pepper, chopped
1 med. tomato, peeled, seeded and chopped
1 sm. red onion, thinly sliced
1 clove garlic, crushed
1/2 t. ground cumin
2 t. chili powder
1/2 t. salt
1 cans tomato sauce
1/2 c. sour cream
2 t. chopped cilantro

In a Crockpot, stir together pork, beans, bell pepper, tomato, onion, garlic, cumin, chili powder, salt, and tomato sauce. Cover and cook on low 8 to 9 hours. Spoon into bowls and top with sour cream and cilantro.

Crockpot Black Bean Soup

2 cans, 15 oz. each, black beans, drained and rinsed
2 cans, 4.5 oz, each, chopped green chiles
1 can, 14.5 oz, Mexican stewed tomatoes, undrained
1 can, 14.5 oz, diced tomatoes, undrained
1 can, 11 oz, whole kernel corn, drained
4 green onions, sliced
2 to 3 t. chili powder
1 tsp. ground cumin
1/2 tsp. dried minced garlic

Combine all ingredients in a 5 qt. crock pot. Cover and cook on high 5 to 6 hours. Makes 8 cups. You can cook it low all day. Serve it with shredded cheddar and fat free sour cream.

Crockpot Black Eyed Peas

1 16 oz bag of dried black-eyed peas
1 small ham hock
1 14 1/2 oz can of diced tomatoes with jalapenos
1 14 1/2 oz can of diced tomatoes with mild green chiles
2 10 1/2 oz cans of chicken broth
1 stalk of celery, chopped
Salt and pepper to taste

Pre-soak black-eyed peas according to the instructions on the bag. Combine all ingredients and cook on low for 8-10 hours.

Crockpot Black Eyed Peas And Okra

2 (16 oz each) packages frozen black eyed peas
2 cups water
1 (15 oz) can ranch style beans with jalapenos undrained
1 cup chopped onion
1 cup chopped green pepper
1 cup chopped celery
1 (12 to 16 oz) package frozen sliced okra
1 can rotel tomatoes and green chilies

Dump all ingredients in crock pot. Cook on low 8 to 10 hours. May take even longer.

Crockpot Boneless Twice Cooked BBQ Ribs

Throw about 1 1/2 lbs of boneless ribs in the crock pot on low with enough water to cover, about 3 tbs of BBQ sauce, fresh chopped garlic, 1/3 cup brown sugar and a couple dashes of ketchup. Cook on low about 5 hours until done. Throw on the BBQ to crisp them up and baste with more BBQ sauce.

Crockpot Boston Baked Beans

1 lb small dry white beans
1 medium onion, chopped
4 slices bacon, chopped
1/4 cup light (mild) molasses
1/4 cup packed dark brown sugar
2 teaspoons dry mustard
1/4 teaspoon ground black pepper
1/8 teaspoon ground cloves
1 1/2 teaspoons salt

Rinse beans with cold running water and discard any stones or shriveled beans. In a large bowl, place beans and enough water to cover by 2 inches. Cover and let stand at room temperature overnight. (Or, in a 6-qt sauce pot, place beans and enough water to cover by 2 inches. heat to boiling over high heat; cook 2 minutes. remove from heat; cover and let stand 1 hour.) Drain and rinse beans.
-in 4 1/2 to 5 1/2 quart Crockpot, stir 3 1/2 cups water with beans and remaining ingredients except salt until blended. Cover crock pot with lid and cook beans on low setting about 14 hours or until beans are tender and sauce is syrupy. Stir salt into bean mixture before serving.

Crockpot Bourbon Breast Of Chicken

4 chicken breasts halves
1/4 c flour
1/2 tsp paprika
Salt
2 tbsp butter
2 tbsp oil
2 tbsp onion, chopped
2 tbsp parsley, chopped
1/4 tsp dried chervil
1/4 c bourbon
1 (4 oz) can mushrooms, undrained
1 (10 oz) can tomatoes
1/4 tsp sugar

Salt & pepper

Dredge chicken in flour which has been mixed with paprika and a little salt. Heat butter and oil in a skillet and sauté chicken on both sides until lightly browned. Stir in onion, parsley and chervil and cook a moment. Remove from heat. Place chicken in crock cooker. Combine remaining ingredients and pour over chicken. Cover and cook on low for 6 to 7 hours. Serve with noodles of rice. Serves 4

Crockpot Broccoli

2 1/2 pounds round steak
1/4 to 1/2" thick
1/2 pound bulk Italian sausage
1 tablespoon dried parsley flakes
1/2 teaspoon leaf oregano
2 cloves garlic -- minced
1 large onion -- finely chopped
1 cans Italian style tomatoes -- 16 0z
1 cans tomato paste -- (6 oz)
1 teaspoon leaf oregano
10 large tomatoes or 2 28 oz cans tomatoes
5 cloves garlic -- chopped
1 tablespoon Worcestershire sauce
2 teaspoons salt
2 large onions -- chopped
1 tablespoon flour
1 tablespoon vegetable oil
1 teaspoon oregano
1 teaspoon thyme
1 tablespoon wine vinegar
1 tablespoon sugar

Trim all excess fat from round steak. Cut into 8 evenly shaped pieces. Pound steak pieces between waxed paper until very thin and easy to roll. In skillet, lightly brown sausage. Drain well and combine with parsley, 1/2 teaspoon oregano, garlic, onion, and salt; mix well. Spread each steak with 2 to 3 tablespoons of sausage mixture. Roll up steaks and tie. Stack steak rolls in crock pot. Combine tomatoes, tomato paste, salt, and 1 teaspoon oregano; pour over rolls. Cover and cook on low setting for 8 to 10 hours. Serve steak rolls with sauce. Sauce: place all ingredients except flour, oil, and vinegar in Crockpot; stir well. Cover and cook on low setting for 8 to 10 hours. Remove cover and turn to high setting for the last hour to reduce excess moisture. Before removing sauce from crock pot, stir in flour, oil, and vinegar. Allow to cool. Pour 3 cups of sauce at a time into blender container; blend until smooth.

Crockpot Braised Chicken Curry With Yams

Canola oil
2 lbs chicken legs and thighs
2 large white onions chopped
1 tbsp minced garlic
1 tbsp minced ginger
1/3 cup madras curry powder (mild, medium/hot your choice)
1 banana
2 bay leaves
4 cups chicken stock
3 large yams, peeled and chopped
Salt and black pepper to taste

In a hot stock pot coated with oil, season the chicken and brown on all sides. Put chicken aside. In the same stockpot, remove all chicken fat, leaving only a coating of oil and sauté onions, garlic and ginger. Caramelize well, and then add curry powder. Mix quickly for 2 minutes making sure not to burn the curry powder. Add back the chicken, banana, bay leaves, yams and chicken stock. Check for seasonings. Bring to a boil and then simmer slowly for 1 1/2 - 2 hours. Serve on basmati rice.

Crockpot Breakfast Casserole

4 medium-sized apples, peeled and sliced
1/4 cup honey
1 tsp. cinnamon
2 tbs. butter, melted
2 cups granola cereal

Place apples in crock pot and mix in remaining ingredients. Cover and cook on low for 7-9 hours (overnight). Serve with milk.

Crockpot Broccoli Soup

4 c. water
4 chicken bouillon cubes
1/4 c. chopped onion
2 c. diced potatoes
1 bag frozen, chopped broccoli
2 cans cream of chicken soup

1/2-1 lb. Velveeta cheese, cubed

Mix water, bouillon cubes, onions, potatoes and broccoli in a crock pot. Cook on high until broccoli is thawed. Add cream of chicken soup and cheese, to taste, to mixture. Turn crock pot on low and cook for 2 hours.

Crockpot Broccoli Soup

4 tablespoons margarine
1/2 cup finely chopped celery
1 cup chopped onion
1 carrots -- thinly sliced (1 to 2)
1 cup water
1/4 cup rice
1/8 teaspoon cayenne pepper
2 heads broccoli (about a pound)
1 can cream of broccoli soup
3 cups 2% low-fat milk
Paprika -- for garnish

Sauté onion, carrot slices and celery in margarine until tender. Stir in water, rice, pepper, and cream of broccoli soup. Stir until smooth. Cover and cook over low to medium heat for 15 minutes. Cut off broccoli stems and slice into very thin pieces - the size of a match stick. Separate tops into florets and steam broccoli until tender. Save a few tops for garnish. Stir broccoli into soup and cook until everything is tender and hot. Now you have a choice. You can place a whole batch of soup into your blender, add the milk and blend until smooth. or, you can put just half the soup in your blender - add the milk and still have some whole pieces of veggies to eat or you can just add the milk and leave all the pieces of veggies alone and enjoy the soup like it is. Anyway, you want to reheat the soup but do not boil. Garnish bowls of soup with paprika and broccoli florets.

Crockpot Brown Rice And Chicken

1 c. diced cooked chicken
2 onions, chopped
2 stalks celery, chopped
2 c. cooked brown rice
1/4 c. dry white wine
2 c. chicken broth
1 c. sliced almonds

Combine all ingredients in crock pot. Cook on low 6 to 8 hours or on automatic 4 to 5 hours. Serve with sliced almonds lightly toasted.

Crockpot Brunch Casserole

1 1/2 lb ground beef
1 ea onion -- large; finely chopped
2 tbsp olive oil or butter
2 ea garlic -- cloves; minced
1 can mushrooms -- sliced; drained; 4 oz
2 tsp salt
1/2 tsp nutmeg
1/2 tsp oregano -- leaf
1/2 pk spinach -- chopped; frozen
3 tbsp flour 6 ea eggs -- beaten
1/4 c milk -- scalded
1/2 c cheddar cheese -- sharp; grated

In skillet, lightly brown ground beef and onion in olive oil; drain well. Place in well-greased crock-pot. Stir in remaining ingredients except eggs, milk and cheese until well blended. Beat eggs and milk together. Pour over other ingredients; stir well. Dust with additional nutmeg. Cover and cook on low setting for 7 to 10 hours or until firm. Just before serving, sprinkle with grated cheese. 6 to 8 servings

Crockpot Cabbage And Beef Casserole

2 lb. ground beef
1 head cabbage, shredded
1 small onion, chopped
1 (16oz) can tomatoes broth or tomato juice to cover bottom of pot
Garlic salt, thyme, red pepper and a bit of oregano

Brown ground beef and drain. Shred cabbage and chop onion. Put in broth or other liquid to cover bottom of pot. Layer cabbage, onion, spices, meat, and garlic salt. Repeat layers ending with beef. Top with tomatoes, undrained and a dusting of oregano. Cook on high for 1 hour. Stir all together. Cook on low heat until ready to eat, 8-10 hours. Makes 3-4 servings.

Crockpot Cabbage Burger Bake

6 cups shredded cabbage and carrots
3/4 pound lean ground beef
1/2 teaspoon salt
1/4 teaspoon ground black pepper

1 medium onion -- finely chopped
1 cup long-grain rice
1 26 oz. can chunky low-fat spaghetti sauce
1/2 cup water
1/4 teaspoon dried basil leaves -- crushed
1/4 teaspoon seasoned salt

Place 1/2 of the cabbage and carrots in a crock pot. Crumble ground beef over top. Sprinkle 1/4 teaspoon of the salt and 1/8 teaspoon of the pepper. Evenly distribute onion, then rice over all. Top with remaining cabbage, salt, and pepper. Combine spaghetti sauce, water, basil, and seasoned salt; pour over cabbage. Cover and cook on low 5 to 6 hours or until rice is tender.

Crockpot Cabbage Chili Soup

3 cups coarsely chopped cabbage
1 cup chopped onions
3 cups healthy choice tomato juice (or any reduced-sodium)
1 (10-1/2 oz) can healthy request tomato soup
10 oz kidney beans, rinsed and drained
2 tsp chili seasoning mix

In a crock pot, combine cabbage, onion, and tomato juice and tomato soup. Add kidney beans and chili seasoning mix. Mix well to combine. Cover and cook on low for 6-8 hours. Mix well before serving. Great recipe for diabetics, dieters.

Crockpot Cafe Chicken

4 lbs cut up chicken
1 onion chopped
2 (or more) cloves of garlic, chopped (not pressed)
1 green pepper chopped
1 medium ripe tomato, peeled & chopped
1 cup dry white wine
Pinch of cayenne pepper

Combine all ingredients in slow-cooker. Cover, set on low and cook for 6-8 hours. If you want you can cook for 5 1/2 and then place chicken on cookie sheets with sides (jelly roll pan) and cook for 30-45 minutes at 350°f to crisp up skin. Serve with crusty French bread. Serves 4-5.

Crockpot Cajun Sausage & Rice

8oz kielbasa sausage cut in 1/4" slices
1 (14 1/2oz) can diced tomatoes with liquid
1 medium onion, diced
1 medium green pepper, diced
2 celery stalks, thinly sliced
1 tbsp chicken bouillon granules
1 tbsp steak sauce
3 bay leaves or 1 tsp dried thyme
1 tsp sugar
1/4 to 1/2 tsp hot pepper sauce
1 cup uncooked instant rice
1/2 cup chopped parsley (optional)

Combine sausage, tomatoes, onion, green pepper, celery bouillon, steak sauce, bay leaves, sugar and hot pepper sauce in Crockpot. Cover and cook on low for 8 hours. Remove bay leaves; stir in rice and 1/2 cup of water. Cook an additional 25 minutes. Stir in parsley if desired. Makes 5 servings

Crockpot Cantonese Dinner

1 1/2 lb pork steak
1/2" thick cut into strips
2 tbsp oil
1 onion large, sliced
1 green pepper small cut into strips
1 4 oz mushroom, drained
1 8 oz tomato sauce can
3 tbsp brown sugar
1 1/2 tbsp vinegar
1 1/2 tsp salt
2 tsp Worcestershire sauce

Brown pork in oil in skillet. Drain on double paper towel. Place pork strips and all remaining ingredients into crock pot. Cover and cook on low for 6 to 8 hr (high 4 hr) serve over hot fluffy rice.

Crockpot Cantonese Pork Dinner

2 pounds pork steaks
2 tablespoons vegetable oil
1 onion, thinly sliced

1 (4.5 ounce) can mushrooms, drained
1 (8 ounce) can tomato sauce
3 tablespoons brown sugar
1 1/2 teaspoons distilled white vinegar
1 1/2 teaspoons salt
2 tablespoons Worcestershire sauce

In a heavy skillet, heat oil over medium high heat. Add pork strips and brown. Drain off excess fat. Place meat, onion, mushrooms, tomato sauce, brown sugar, vinegar, salt, and Worcestershire sauce in a crock pot. Cook on high for 4 hours or on low for 6 to 8 hours. Serve hot.

Crockpot Caponata

1 lb plum tomatoes chopped
1 eggplant in 1/2" pieces
2 med zucchini in 1/2" pieces
1 onion finely chopped
3 stalks celery sliced
1/2 c chopped parsley
2 tbsp red wine vinegar
1 tbsp brown sugar
1/4 c raisins
1/4 c tomato paste
1 tsp salt
1/4 tsp freshly ground black pepper
3 tbsp oil cured black olives (optional)
2 tbsp capers (optional)

Combine tomatoes, eggplant, zucchini, celery, onion, parsley, vinegar, sugar, raisins, tomato paste, salt & pepper in crock pot. Cook, covered on low heat for 5 1/2 hours. Do not remove cover during cooking. Stir in olives & capers, if using. Serve warm or cold.

Crockpot Caramel Apple Euphoria Dessert

2 med cooking apples
1/2 c apple juice
7 oz caramel candy squares
1 tsp vanilla
1/8 tsp ground cardamom
1/2 tsp ground cinnamon
1/3 c cream-style peanut butter

7 slice angel-food cake; or
1 qt vanilla ice cream

Peel, core, and cut each apple into 18 wedges; set aside. Combine apple juice, unwrapped caramel candies, vanilla, cardamom and cinnamon. Drop peanut butter 1 teaspoon at a time, over ingredients in Crockpot. Stir. Add apple wedges; cover and cook on low for 5 hours. Stir thoroughly; cover and cook on low 1 additional hour. Serve approximately 1/3 cup of warm mixture over a slice of angel food cake or ice cream. Serves 7.

Crockpot Caramel Apples

2 packages (14oz) bags caramels
1/4 cup water
8 medium apples

In Crockpot, combine caramels and water. Cover and cook on high for 1 to 1 1/2 hours, stirring frequently. Wash and dry apples. Insert stick into stem end of each apple. Turn control on low. Dip apple into hot caramel and turn to coat entire surface. Holding apple above pot, scrape off excess accumulation of caramel from bottom apple. Place on greased wax paper to cool.

Crockpot Caramel Pie

2 packages (14 oz) bags caramels
1/4 cup water
8 medium apples

In Crockpot, combine caramels and water. Cover and cook on high for 1 to 1 1/2 hours, stirring frequently. Wash and dry apples. Insert stick into stem end of each apple. Turn control on low. Dip apple into hot caramel and turn to coat entire surface. Holding apple above pot, scrape off excess accumulation of caramel from bottom apple. Place on greased wax paper to cool.

Crockpot Caramel Rum Fondue

7 ounces caramels
1/4 cup miniature marshmallows
1/3 cup whipping cream
2 teaspoons rum or 1/4 t rum extract

Combine caramels and cream in crock pot. Cover and heat until melted, 30 to 60 minutes. Stir in marshmallows and rum. Cover and continue cooking 30 minutes. Serve with apple wedges or pound cake.

Crockpot Carne Gisada

3 lbs beef stew meat
2 cans diced rotel tomatoes with green chilies
Salt and pepper to taste
3 cloves garlic minced
1 cup chopped onion
3 tbsp flour
1/2 tsp cumin
1/2 tsp oregano
1 tsp chili powder
1/4 cup water
1 diced bell pepper

Place stew meat, 1/4 cup water, salt and pepper in Crockpot. Turn heat to high and let simmer for 1 1/2 hours. Drain juice from tomatoes into measuring cup. Add tomatoes garlic and onions to crock pot stir let simmer on high for 30 minutes. Add cumin, oregano, and chili powder to crock pot and stir. Blend juice and enough water to equal 1 1/2 cups liquid and flour stir into meat/veggie mixture. Let cook on low for 3-4 hours until sauce is nice and thick (if you like runnier gravy three hours is good) serve with warm flour tortillas.

Crockpot Carrot Chicken

Skinless, boneless chicken breasts
1 medium head cabbage, quartered
1 pound carrots cut into 1" pieces
Water to cover
4 cubes chicken bouillon
1 teaspoon poultry seasoning
1/4 teaspoon Greek-style seasoning
2 tablespoons cornstarch
1/4 cup water

Rinse chicken and place in crock pot. Rinse cabbage and place on top of chicken, and then add carrots. Add enough water to almost cover all. Add bouillon cubes and sprinkle liberally with poultry seasoning. Add Greek seasoning to taste (as you would salt and pepper). Cook on low for 8 hours or on high for 4 hours. To make gravy: when you're nearly ready to eat, pour off some of the juice and place in a saucepan. Bring to a boil. Dissolve cornstarch in about 1/4 cup water (depending on how thick you like your gravy). Add to saucepan and simmer all together until thick. If desired, season with additional Greek seasoning. Serve gravy over chicken and potatoes, if desired.

Crockpot Catalina Ribs

1 1/2-2 lbs boneless pork ribs
1 onion chopped
2 cloves garlic, minced
1 (8 oz) bottle of Catalina

Place or throw ribs in crock pot. Put in rest of ingredients and cook low for 5-7 hours.

Crockpot Cheese And Meatball Soup

2 cups water
1 cup corn -- whole kernel
1 cup potato -- chopped
1 cup celery -- chopped
1/2 cup carrot -- sliced
1/2 cup onion -- chopped
2 cubes beef bouillon
1 jar cheez whiz -- (16 oz)
1 pound ground beef
1/4 cup bread crumbs
1 large egg
1/2 teaspoon salt
1/2 teaspoon Tabasco sauce

Meatballs: mix ingredients together thoroughly. Shape into medium size meatballs. Place uncooked meatballs and all other ingredients, except cheez whiz, in electric crock pot. Stir gently. Cover and cook on setting # 2 (low) for 8 to 10 hours. Before serving add cheez whiz, stirring gently until well blended.

Crockpot Cheese Dip

2 lb. Velveeta cheese
2 cans rotel tomatoes and chilies
1 can cream of mushroom soup
1 sm. jar picante sauce
1 tsp. garlic powder
Dash of Worcestershire
1 lb. premium ground beef
1 med. onion, chopped
1 lb. sausage

Mix all of the liquids and cheese together in a crock pot set on low until the cheese melts. While this is cooking, brown meats and chopped onion. Drain grease off of meats and add spices, then add to crock pot and stir. Cook on low 2 to 4 hours; keep on low to serve with chips and crackers.

Crockpot Cheese Fondue

10-oz. cans cheddar cheese soup
1 lb block process cheese spread cut in 8 pieces
1 lb Swiss cheese, grated
12-oz. cans beer (or apple cider)
1/2 tsp hot pepper sauce
2 drops liquid smoke flavoring

Place all ingredients in crock pot. Stir to mix. Cover and cook on low for 2 hours. After 1 hour of cooking time, stir. Before serving, whisk to blend. Serve with bread sticks or veggies for dipping.

Crockpot Cheese Soufflé

14 slices fresh white bread, crust removed
3 c. grated sharp cheese, cheddar
1/4 c. oleo
6 lg. eggs
3 c. milk, scalded
2 tbsp. Worcestershire sauce
1/2 tsp. salt paprika

Tear bread in small pieces. Place 1/2 in well greased crock pot. Add 1/2 cheese, 1/2 butter. Add remaining bread, cheese and butter. Beat eggs, milk, Worcestershire sauce and salt. Pour over bread and cheese. Sprinkle with paprika. Cover and cook on low 4-6 hours. Do not open until ready to serve.

Crockpot Cheese Soup

1/2 stick butter
3 green onions -- chopped
3 stalks celery with leaves -- chopped
2 carrots -- grated
2 cans chicken broth
2 cans cheese soup
1 can cream of potato soup
Parsley flakes

Tabasco sauce -- to taste
Salt and pepper -- to taste
8 ounces sour cream/or plain nonfat yogurt
3 tablespoons cooking sherry

Melt butter over low heat and sauté onions, celery and carrots. Add chicken broth; cover and simmer for 30 minutes. Add other soups, parsley, Tabasco, salt & pepper. Stir in sour cream. Simmer 15 minutes. Add sherry and stir before serving.

Crockpot Cheesy Bacon Dip

2 pkgs (8 oz) cream cheese, softened, cut into cubes
4 cups shredded Colby-jack cheese
1 cup half-and-half
2 t mustard
1 t chopped onion
2 tsp Worcestershire sauce
1/2 tsp salt
1/4 tsp hot pepper sauce
1 lb bacon, cooked and crumbled

Place cream cheese, Colby-jack cheese, half-and-half, mustard, onion, Worcestershire sauce, salt and pepper sauce in crock pot. Cover and cook, stirring occasionally, on low 1 hour or until cheese melts. Stir in bacon; adjust seasonings. Serve with crusty bread or crackers.

Crockpot Cheesy Chicken Ala Tiffany

1 can mushroom soup
1 can cream of broccoli soup
1 cans broccoli cheese soup
2 pkgs chicken breasts (boneless, skinless)
1 can mixed vegetables
1-2 t tapioca for thickening
1 cup shredded cheddar cheese

Dice chicken put in Crockpot sprinkle with salt and pepper, pour all three cans of soup over chicken and stir. Cover and cook on low about 4-6 hours. About an hour before serving add mixed vegetables, cheese and thicken with tapioca.

Crockpot Cheesy Creamed Corn

3 16 oz. pkgs frozen corn
1 8 oz. pkg cream cheese
1 3 oz. pkg cream cheese
4 tbsp butter
3 tbsp water
3 tbsp milk
2 tbsp sugar
6 slices American cheese

Combine all ingredients in crock pot, mix well. Cover and cook 4 - 5 hours on low, or until heated through and cheese is melted. Stir well before serving.

Crockpot Chicken I

1 frying chicken, cut up
Salt & pepper
1 can cream of mushroom soup
1/2 c. sauterne or sherry
2 tbsp. butter or margarine, melted
2 tbsp. dry Italian salad dressing mix
2 (3 oz.) pkgs. cream cheese, cut in cubes
1 tbsp. onion, chopped

Wash chicken and pat dry. Brush with butter. Sprinkle with salt and pepper. Place in crock pot. Sprinkle with dry salad mix. Cover and cook on low for 5 to 6 hours. About 3/4 hour before serving, mix soup, cream cheese, wine, and onion in small saucepan. Cook until smooth. Pour over chicken in pot. Cover and cook for 30 minutes on low. Serve with sauce. Serve with rice or noodles. Serves 4 to 6.

Crockpot Chicken II

1 large chicken, cut-up
2 c. soy sauce
2 c. vinegar

Put in Crockpot and cook on high 4-5 hours.

Crockpot Chicken Ala King

1 can cream of chicken soup
3 tbsp. flour

1/4 tsp.
Pepper
Dash of cayenne pepper
1 lb. boneless, skinless chicken breasts cut into cubes
1 celery rib, chopped
1/2 c. chopped green pepper
1/4 c. chopped onion
1 package (10 oz.) frozen peas, thawed
2 tbsp. diced pimentos, drained
Hot cooked rice

Combine soup, flour and peppers in crock pot, stir until smooth. Stir in chicken, celery, onion and green pepper. Cover and cook on low 7-8 hours or until meat is cooked through. Stir in peas and pimentos. Cook 30 minutes longer. Serve over rice.

Crockpot Chicken And Dumplings

4 tablespoons butter
1 tablespoon vegetable oil
1 onion -- chopped
3 pounds your favorite chicken parts -- cut up
2 cups chicken broth
2 stalks celery
1 tablespoon minced parsley
2 carrots -- peeled, sliced
1 tsp black pepper
Salt to taste
1/2 tsp ground allspice
1 cup dry white wine (optional but really adds a nice taste)
1 can refrigerate biscuits
1/2 cup heavy cream
2 tablespoons flour

In a large skillet, brown onion in butter and oil just until tender, then brown chicken parts and place all in a 6-quart Crockpot. Add remaining ingredients except heavy cream, flour and biscuits. Cook on high 2-1/2 to 3 hours, or on low 5 to 7 hours. When chicken is done, remove pieces to plate and let cool, then debone. While chicken is cooling, mix flour and cream together, then stir into Crockpot. Open biscuits and cut each biscuit into 4 pieces. Drop into Crockpot and turn on high. These will need to cook about 30 minutes, until they are firm. Return chicken meat to Crockpot after deboning and serve. You can use your own homemade biscuit recipe for canned if you prefer.

Crockpot Chicken & Noodles

4 carrots, sliced
4-5 pieces chicken
1 small onion, chopped
2 cups water
4 chicken bouillon cubes
1 tsp garlic
Salt & pepper, to taste
1 lb egg noodles

Place carrots in crock pot, followed by all ingredients except noodles. Cook on low for 8 hours. At the end of cooking time, cook egg noodles on stovetop. While noodles cook, remove chicken from crock pot & cut into bite-size pieces. Return chicken & noodles to crock pot. If desired, thicken broth with cornstarch & water. Just be sure to add some of the broth to your cornstarch mixture first. This will prevent any lumps from forming.

Crockpot Chicken And Pasta

1 t cooking oil
1 lb boneless skinless chicken breasts (cut into bite sized pieces)
1 can of cream of chicken soup
1/2 cup water
1 bag frozen seasoned pasta and veggie combo

Heat the oil and then brown the chicken in it. Set the chicken aside and add soup, water, and the pasta/veggie combo. Heat to a boil. Return the chicken to the pan and reduce the heat to low. Cover and cook for 5 min. or until the chicken is no longer pink. Stir occasionally. Serves about 4.

Crockpot Chicken And Rice I

Boneless, skinless chicken breast (2-3 lbs)
Chicken flavored rice
Cream of celery soup
Cream of chicken soup
1 cup water
Salt

Put rice in Crockpot, and water. Combine soups and layer on top of rice. Salt chicken and layer chicken in pot. Set on high for 4-5 hours or low or auto shift for 7-10 hours.

Crockpot Chicken And Rice II

3/4 c. rice
1 can cream of celery soup
1 can cream of mushroom soup
1 sm. can whole mushrooms
1 sm. jar pimento strips, drained
1/2 green pepper, chopped
1/2 onion, chopped
1 can water chestnuts, drained, sliced
8 to 12 chicken breasts, halved
Grated parmesan cheese

Place rice in crock pot. Combine remaining ingredients except chicken and cheese in bowl. Mix well. Pour half of mixture over rice. Place chicken on top. Pour remaining soup mixture over all. Cook on high for 3 hours or until chicken is tender. Garnish with cheese.

Crockpot Chicken And Sausage Paella

2 1/2 to 3 lbs. meaty chicken pieces
1 tbsp. cooking oil
8 oz. cooked smoked turkey sausage, halved lengthwise and sliced
1 large onion, sliced
3 cloves garlic, minced
2 tbsp. snipped fresh thyme or 2 tsp. dried thyme, crushed
1/4 tsp. black pepper
1/8 tsp. thread saffron or
1/4 tsp. ground turmeric
1 141/2 oz. can reduce chicken broth
1/2 c. water
2 c. chopped tomatoes
2 yellow or green sweet peppers cut into very thin bite-size strips
1 c. frozen green peas
3 c. hot cooked rice

Skin chicken. Rinse chicken; pat dry. In a large skillet brown chicken pieces, half at a time, in hot oil. Drain off fat. In a 3 1/2, 4, or 5 quart crockery cooker place chicken pieces, turkey sausage, and onion. Sprinkle with garlic, dried thyme (if using), black pepper, and saffron or turmeric. Pour broth and water overall. Cover; cook on low-heat setting for 7 to 8 hours or on high-heat setting for 3 1/2 to 4 hours. Add the tomatoes, sweet peppers, peas, and if using, the fresh thyme to the cooker. Cover; let stand for 5 minutes. Serve over the hot rice. Makes 6 servings.

Crockpot Chicken Cacciatore 1

1 large onion, thinly sliced
1 1/2 lb. skinless, boneless chicken breasts
2 (6 oz each) cans tomato paste
8 oz. fresh sliced mushrooms
1/2 tsp. salt
1/4 tsp. pepper
2 cloves garlic, minced
1 tsp. oregano
1/2 tsp. basil
1 bay leaf
1/4 c. dry white wine
1/4 c. water

Put sliced onion in bottom of crock pot. Add chicken pieces. Stir together tomato paste, mushrooms, salt, pepper, garlic, herbs, white wine and water. Spread over chicken. Cover; cook on low 7 to 9 hours (high: 3 to 4 hours). Serve chicken pieces over hot spaghetti or vermicelli. 4 servings.

Crockpot Chicken Cacciatore II

1 chicken (5 pounds), cut into pieces
1/4 cup olive oil
1 cup flour
1 cup chopped onions
1 cup sliced mushrooms
1 cup julienned carrot
1 cup julienned green pepper
2 tablespoons minced garlic
8 cups chopped, peeled tomatoes
1/2 cup tomato paste
3/4 cup red or Marsala wine
1 teaspoon oregano
1 teaspoon basil
1 1/2 teaspoons salt
1 teaspoon pepper freshly grated
Romano cheese

Wash and drain the chicken pieces. Heat the oil in a deep skillet. Roll and coat each chicken piece in the flour and brown each piece on all sides to a golden brown. Transfer the chicken to paper towels to drain. Sauté the onion, mushrooms, carrots, green peppers, and garlic in the same skillet for 10 minutes. Add the tomatoes and sauté for another 5 minutes. Stir in the tomato paste, wine, herbs, salt and pepper, and cook over medium heat for another 5 minutes. Add all the chicken pieces and mix well. Turn down the heat very low, and simmer, covered, for 1 hour. Adjust the salt and pepper to your taste. Serve with some freshly grated cheese and a nice warm loaf of Italian bread.

Crockpot Chicken Cacciatore III

1 can tomatoes, diced
2 cans (small ones) tomato paste
1/2 c. dry white wine
1 can mushrooms
1 small onion, sliced
4 cloves garlic, sliced
1 tbsp Italian seasoning
1 tsp basil
1 tsp oregano
Mix all those together and pour it over the top of the chicken. Then cook on low 7-8 hours.

Crockpot Chicken Casserole

4 lg. chicken breasts
1 sm. can cream of chicken soup
1 sm. can cream of celery soup
1 sm. can cream of mushroom soup
1/2 c. diced celery
1 c. minute rice

Mix in Crockpot the soups and rice. Place chicken on top of mixture, then sprinkle diced celery over chicken. Cook on low for 4 hours. Makes 4 servings.

Crockpot Chicken Cordon Bleu

4-6 chicken breasts (pounded out thin)
4-6 pieces of ham
4-6 slices of Swiss cheese
1 can cream of mushroom soup
1/4 c. milk

Put ham and cheese on chicken. Roll up and secure with a toothpick. Place chicken in crock pot so it looks like a triangle; layer the rest on top. Mix soup and milk. Pour over top of chicken. Cover and cook on low for 4 hours or until chicken is no longer pink. Serve over noodles with the sauce it makes.

Crockpot Chicken And Dumplings

4 tablespoons butter
1 tablespoon vegetable oil
1 onion -- chopped
3 pounds your favorite chicken parts -- cut up
2 cups chicken broth
2 stalks celery
1 tablespoon minced parsley
2 carrots -- peeled, sliced
1 tsp black pepper
Salt to taste
1/2 tsp ground allspice
1 cup dry white wine (optional but really adds a nice taste)
1 can refrigerate biscuits
1/2 cup heavy cream
2 tablespoons flour

In a large skillet, brown onion in butter and oil just until tender, then brown chicken parts and place all in a 6-quart Crockpot. Add remaining ingredients except heavy cream, flour and biscuits. Cook on high 2-1/2 to 3 hours, or on low 5 to 7 hours. When chicken is done, remove pieces to plate and let cool, then debone. While chicken is cooling, mix flour and cream together, then stir into Crockpot. Open biscuits and cut each biscuit into 4 pieces. Drop into Crockpot and turn on high. These will need to cook about 30 minutes, until they are firm.

Crockpot Chicken Enchiladas I

Boneless, skinless chicken (can still be frozen)
1 large can enchilada sauce (green or red)
Medium or large flour tortillas
Shredded cheese

Empty enchilada sauce into the Crockpot and place chicken filets into the sauce. Cook on low setting all day. Scoop out chicken and cut or shred onto a plate. Spread a tortilla on another plate and arrange some chicken into a "stripe" down the middle. Sprinkle liberal shredded cheese, and ladle some sauce over it. Roll the tortilla up, ladle more sauce over it, and sprinkle more cheese. Place in the microwave for about 20 seconds on high to melt the cheese. More microwave time maybe needed for multiple enchiladas on one plate.

Crockpot Chicken Enchiladas Ii

1 lg. cans enchilada sauce
4 chicken breasts
2 cans cream of chicken soup
1 sm. can sliced black olives
2 dozen corn tortillas
1 chopped onion
1 pkg sharp cheddar cheese

Cook chicken and shred. Mix soup, olives and onions. Cut tortillas in wedges. Layer Crockpot with sauce, tortillas, soup mix, chicken and cheese all the way to top, ending with cheese on top. Cook on low temp all day.

Crockpot Chicken Fricassee

1 can reduced fat cream of chicken soup
1/2 soup can water
1/2 cup chopped onions
1 teaspoon paprika
1 teaspoon lemon juice
1 teaspoon rosemary
1 teaspoon thyme
1 teaspoon salt
1/4 teaspoon pepper
4 skinless boneless chicken breast
Non-stick cooking spray

Spray Crockpot with non-stick cooking spray. Place chicken in Crockpot. Mix remaining ingredients together and pour over chicken. Cover and cook on low 6-8 hours.

1 hour before serving, prepare chive dumplings:
3 tbsp. shortening
1 1/2 cups flour
2 tsp. baking powder
3/4 tsp. salt
3 tbsp fresh, chopped chives, or 2 tbsp. dried chives
3/4 cup skim milk

Mix dry ingredients and shortening. Add chives and milk, combine well. Drop by teaspoonfuls onto hot chicken and gravy. Cover and cook on high for 45-60 minutes. Serve with mashed potatoes and vegetables, or over hot, cooked noodles.

Crockpot Chicken Fried Chops

1/2 cups all purpose flour
2 tsp salt
1 1/2 tsp ground mustard
1/2 tsp garlic powder
6 pork chops, trimmed
2 tbsp vegetable oil
1 cans condensed cream of chicken soup, undiluted
1/3 cup water

In a shallow bowl, combine flour, salt, mustard and garlic powder; dredge pork chops. In a skillet, brown the chops on both sides in oil. Place in a crock pot or Crockpot. Combine soup and water; pour over chops. Cover and cook on low for 6-8 hours or until meat is tender. If desired, thicken pan juices and serve with the pork chops.

Crockpot Chicken In A Pot

3 lb whole chicken
2 carrots, sliced
2 onions, sliced
2 celery stalks with leaves
1 tsp basil
2 tsp salt
1/2 tsp black pepper
1/2 c chicken broth or wine

Put carrots, onions, and celery in bottom of crock-pot. Add whole chicken. Top with salt, pepper, liquid. Sprinkle basil over top. Cover and cook until done-low 8 to 10 hours. (High 3 to 4 hours, using 1 cup water). Remove chicken and vegetables with spatula.

Crockpot Chicken In Spicy Sauce

1/2 cup tomato juice
1/2 cup soy sauce
1/2 cup brown sugar
1/4 cup chicken broth
3 cloves garlic minced
1 whole chicken, cut in skinless serving size pieces or favorite parts

Combine all ingredients except chicken in a bowl. Dip each piece of chicken in the sauce. Place in the crock pot. Pour remaining sauce over the top. Cook on low for 6-8 hours or high 3-4 hours. Makes 6 servings.

Crockpot Chicken N Noodles

2 1/2 to 3 1/2 pound broiler/fryer chicken cut up
1 cup chicken broth
2 cups water
1 package (8 ounces) egg noodles
Salt and pepper to taste

Place chicken in crock-pot. Season with salt and pepper; add all liquid. Cover and cook on low 8 to 10 hours (high 4 to 5 hours) remove chicken from broth. Turn Crockpot to high and add noodles. Bone chicken and cut up meat. Stir chicken into noodles. Cover and cook 30 to 45 minutes, stirring occasionally.

Crockpot Chicken Noodle Soup New Orleans Style

1 lg whole fryer
1/2 c diced celery
4 ea cloves minced garlic
3 ea bay leaves
4 ea qts water
2 tbsp butter
1 c sliced mushrooms
1/4 c cream sherry
Green onions for garnish
1 c diced onions
1/2 c minced parsley
1 c chopped carrots
1 tsp poultry seasoning
12 oz broad egg noodles
1 c sliced onion rings
1 c diced carrots
Salt and pepper to taste

First, take the chicken and wash it thoroughly - that means both inside and out! Remove the giblets, scrub out the internal cavity under cold running water, and scrape away anything that doesn't look edible. (But do not remove the chicken skin or any of the fat! you need the skin to make a rich stock.) Next, take a crock pot and place the chicken and giblets into it. then drop in the diced onions, the 1/2 cup of chopped carrots and bay leaves, poultry seasoning and *2* quarts of water. Then, with a spoon, evenly distribute the seasoning mixture around the chicken, turn the crock pot to high, and cook for at least six hours (or better still, overnight). Remember, the longer you cook, the richer the base stock and the more tender the chicken. While the chicken is slow-cooking, it's a good time to prepare your noodles. Go ahead and boil them according to package ... but do not cook them until done! Keep in mind that you're going to drop them into a soup, so you want them el dente (firm), otherwise they'll turn to pure mush by the time you eat them. Furthermore, you want a small percent of the starch in the noodles to cook into the soup to thicken it slightly - if you cook the noodles all the way, the soup's consistency will be flat and thin. After the noodles are cooked, butter them slightly and set them aside. When the chicken is tender, take a set of tongs or a strainer spoon, remove it from the crock pot (it may tend to fall apart, but that's okay), and set it on a platter to cool. At this point, strain out all the seasoning vegetables from the stock, place the stock into a metal bowl, and place the bowl into the refrigerator or freezer until the chicken fat congeals (which should take about 1 hour). Meanwhile, pick the chicken off the bones and, with a sharp knife, chop it into bite-sized pieces. Then, in a heavy 12-inch skillet, melt the butter and sauté the sliced onions, mushrooms, and carrots until they're tender. Then drop in the chopped chicken meat. And over medium-low heat, cook it into the vegetables for about 10 minutes. While the chicken and vegetables are sautéing, remove the chicken stock from the refrigerator, skim off all the fat, and place the skimmed stock into a soup pot, along with the remaining 2 quarts of water. At this point, you should season the soup stock to taste with salt and pepper. Now drop in the sautéed chicken, mushrooms, onion rings and diced carrots - along with the sherry, the Tabasco, and as soon as it comes to a boil, reduce the heat to low and simmer the soup about 30 minutes to allow all the flavors to thoroughly blend. When you're ready to eat, ladle out heaping helpings of the piping hot soup into bowls, garnish with a sprinkling of thinly sliced green onions, and serve with crunch saltines.

Crockpot Chicken Noodle Soup

3 carrots, peeled and cut into chunks
3 stalks celery, cut into chunks
1 large onion, quartered
3 boneless skinless chicken breast halves
2 cans chicken broth Swanson's healthy request, fat free
2 to 3 soup cans of water
Generous shake of dried dill
Generous shake of dried parsley
8 oz. noodles

Put vegetables in crock pot. Add chicken. Pour in broth and water. Add dill and parsley. Cover and cook on low 8 hours. Remove veggies and chicken from crock pot. Add noodles, turn to high and heat while you shred the chicken and mince the veggies. Return chicken and veggies to crock pot and heat through. It takes the noodles about 20 minute to cook. Serves 6.

Crockpot Chicken Noodle Soup (Low Fat)

3 carrots, peeled and cut into chunks
3 stalks celery, cut into chunks
1 large onion, quartered
3 boneless skinless chicken breast halves
2 cans chicken broth Swanson's healthy request, fat free
2 to 3 soup cans of water
Generous shake of dried dill
Generous shake of dried parsley
8 oz. noodles

Put vegetables in crock pot. Add chicken. Pour in broth and water. Add dill and parsley. Cover and cook on low 8 hours. Remove veggies and chicken from crock pot. Add noodles, turn to high and heat while you shred the chicken and mince the veggies. Return chicken and veggies to crock pot and heat through. It takes the noodles about 20 minutes to cook. Serves 6.

Crockpot Chicken Parmigiana

3 chicken breasts
1 egg
1 t salt
1/4 tsp pepper
1 c dry bread crumbs
1 1/4 c butter
1 cans pizza sauce -- 10 1/2 oz
6 slices mozzarella cheese
Parmesan cheese

If using whole chicken breasts, cut in to halves. In bowl beat egg salt and pepper dip chicken into egg. Then coat with crumbs. In large skillet sauté chicken in butter. Arrange chicken in pot. Pour pizza sauce over chicken. Cover and cook on low 6 to 8 hours. Add mozzarella cheese, sprinkle parmesan cheese on top. Cover and cook 15 minutes. Makes 6 servings.

Crockpot Chicken Parmigiana & Eggplant

3 chicken breasts
1 small egg plant sliced
1 egg
10 1/2 oz can pizza sauce
1 tsp salt
6 slices mozzarella cheese

1/4 tsp pepper
1 c dry bread crumbs
1/2 c butter

If using whole chicken breasts, cut into halves. In a bowl beat egg, salt, and pepper. Dip chicken into the egg, then coat with crumbs. In a large skillet or Crockpot with a browning unit, sauté chicken in the butter. Arrange eggplant and the chicken in pot, (place eggplant on the bottom or it will not cook completely.) pour pizza sauce over the chicken. Cover and cook on low 6 to 8 hours. Add mozzarella cheese; sprinkle parmesan cheese on top. Cover and cook 15 minutes.

Crockpot Chicken Pizza

4 skinless, boneless chicken breast- cut into bite size pieces
1 onion, chopped
1 green bell pepper, chopped
2 large cans tomato sauce
2 large cans diced tomatoes
1 tablespoon dried parsley
1 tablespoon dried oregano
1 tablespoon dried basil
1 tsp. thyme
4 cloves garlic, pressed
1 bay leaf

Place all ingredients in crock pot. Stir to make sure all chicken is coated well. Cook on low setting for 8 hours, until chicken and vegetables are tender.

Crockpot Chicken/Sausage Cassoulet

1 package frozen lima beans
1 cup tomato juice
1 carrot -- 1/2 inch pcs
1 stalk celery -- ½ inch pcs
1 onion -- chopped
1 clove garlic -- minced
1 bay leaf
1 teaspoon chicken bouillon granules
1/2 teaspoon dried basil -- crushed
1/2 teaspoon dried oregano -- crushed
3 boneless chicken breasts
3 chicken drumsticks

8 ounces smoked kielbasa

Place carrots, limas, celery and onions on bottom of Crockpot which has been sprayed with pam. combine herbs, juice and bouillon and add to vegetables. Place chicken on top of vegetables. Cut sausage into pieces. Put chicken and sausage on top of vegetables cover Crockpot and cook on low heat for 10 hours or on high for 5 hours. Remove bay leaf before serving.

Crockpot Chicken Soup

2 carrots
2 celery stalks
2 onions
3 boneless, skinless chicken breast
2 tsp salt
1/2 tsp pepper
4 cups chicken broth
4 to 5 cups water
1 t dried parsley
1 t dried dill
6 oz noodles

Slice carrots, celery and onion. Place in crock pot. Add chicken, broth, water, and spices. Cover and cook on low 8 to 10 hours. One hour before serving, remove chicken and vegetables from pot. Add 6oz. noodles to pot cover and turn to high. While noodles are cooking, shred the chicken and mince the vegetables. Return chicken and veggies to the pot. Cook till noodles are done.

Crockpot Chicken Stew

2 lb chicken breasts/skinless boneless/ cut in 1" cubes
2 c fat-free chicken broth
3 c potatoes; peel, cube
1 c onion; chop
1 c celery; sliced
1 c carrots; sliced thin
1 tsp paprika
1/2 tsp pepper
1/2 tsp rubbed sage
1/2 tsp dried thyme
6 oz no-salt-added tomato paste
1/4 c cold water

3 tbsp cornstarch

In a crock pot, combine the first 11 ingredients; cover and cook on high for 4 hours. Mix water and cornstarch until smooth; stir into stew. Cook, covered, 30 minutes more or until the vegetables are tender.

Crockpot Chicken Stew Mexican Style

2 lbs skinless boneless chicken breasts cut into 1 1/2" pieces
4 med russet potatoes, peeled and cut very small
1 (15 oz) can mild salsa
1 (4 oz) can diced green chilies
1 (1 1/4 oz) pkg taco seasoning mix
1 (8oz) can tomato sauce

Mix all ingredients together in Crockpot; cook 7-9 hours on low. Serve with warm flour tortillas. You can also served corn with this. It is good mixed in it too.

Crockpot Chicken Stroganoff

1 cup sour cream
1 tablespoon gold medal all-purpose flour
1 envelope (.87 to 1.2 oz) chicken gravy mix
1 cup water
1 lb. boneless, skinless chicken breast halves, cut into 1" pieces
1 16 oz. bag frozen stew vegetables, thawed
1 4-oz. jar sliced mushrooms, drained
1 cup frozen peas, thawed
1 1/2 cups bisquick original or reduced fat baking mix
4 green onions, chopped
1/2 cup milk

Mix sour cream, flour, gravy mix and water in 3 1/2 to 4-quart crock pot until smooth. Stir in chicken, stew vegetables and mushrooms. Cover and cook on low heat setting 4 hours or until chicken is tender and sauce is thickened. Stir in peas. Mix baking mix and onions. Stir in milk just until moistened. Drop dough by rounded tablespoonfuls onto chicken-vegetable mixture. Cover and cook on high heat setting 45 to 50 minutes or until toothpick inserted in center of dumplings comes out clean. Serve immediately.

Crockpot Chicken Thighs

6 chicken thighs (remove skin)
1 cans Italian-style diced tomatoes (28 oz)
Salt and pepper
Throw these in the Crockpot and cook on high for about 3 hours. Serve with egg noodles.

Crockpot Chicken Tortillas

Meat from 1 whole chicken or canned chicken or parts
1 can cream of chicken soup
1/2 c. green chili salsa
2 tbsp. quick cooking tapioca
1 med. onion, chopped
1 1/2 c. grated cheese
1 doz. corn tortillas
Black olives

Tear chicken into bite size pieces; mix with soup, chili, salsa and tapioca. Line bottom of crock pot with 3 corn tortillas, torn into bite size pieces. Add 1/3 of the chicken mixture. Sprinkle with 1/3 of the onion and 1/3 of the grated cheese. Repeat layers of tortillas topped with chicken mixture, onions and cheese. Cover and cook on low 6 to 8 hours or high for 3 hours. Garnish with sliced black olives.

Crockpot Chicken Wings

5 lb. chicken wings
2 c. brown sugar
1 c. French's mustard
4 tbsp. soy sauce

Cut each wing into 3 pieces - throw away the tip. Brown in skillet until golden brown and put in crock pot, turn on low heat. Mix brown sugar, mustard and soy sauce in saucepan and heat until it becomes liquid. Pour over the wings and cook 2-8 hours.

Crockpot Chicken With Cheese Sauce

Place two chicken breast halves in Crockpot (frozen or thawed). Mix together one can cream of chicken soup & half soup can of white wine; pour over chicken. Place two slices Swiss cheese over top of chicken breasts (processed cheese melts and blends more easily). Cook in Crockpot for 2-3 hours (on high) or 3-4 hours (on low). Serve over steamed rice

Crockpot Chili I

2 onions, chopped
2 cloves garlic
1 lb. lean hamburger
2 tbs. chili powder
Cumin to taste
2 cans (16 oz. ea.) tomatoes
2 cans tomato soup
2 cans kidney beans, drained
Salt and pepper to taste
Optional: shredded cheese and/or sour cream for topping

Cook onions and garlic in 2 tbs. oil till onions are yellow. Add hamburger and cook till browned. Stir in chili powder and optional cumin; cook 2 minutes more. Meanwhile, in Crockpot, combine remaining ingredients. Stir in browned meat mixture. Cover and cook on low setting for 8-10 hours. To serve: ladle chili into bowls. Top with optional shredded cheese and/or sour cream, if desired.

Crockpot Chili II

1 lb ground beef, cooked and rinsed
60-70 ounces rinsed light or dark kidney beans
16 ounces tomato paste
16 ounces peeled chopped tomatoes (reserve liquid)
1/2 small onion, chopped
1 small green pepper, chopped
1 package chili seasonings
Cayenne pepper to taste, if desired

Put it all in the Crockpot and cook on low until you are ready.

Crockpot Chili III

1 16 oz can kidney beans -- drained
2 14 1/2 oz can tomatoes
2 pounds ground chuck -- coarsely ground
2 medium onions -- coarsely chopped
1 green pepper -- coarsely chopped
2 cloves garlic -- crushed
3 tablespoons chili powder
1 teaspoon pepper

1 teaspoon cumin

Salt to taste

Put all ingredients in crock pot in order listed. Stir once. Cover and cook on low 10-12 hours.

Crockpot Chili Con Carne

4 pounds ground beef
3 tablespoons shortening
2 cups chopped onion
2 garlic cloves -- crushed
4 tablespoons chili powder
3 beef bouillon cubes -- crushed
1 1/2 teaspoons paprika
1 teaspoon oregano
1 teaspoon ground cumin
1/2 teaspoon cayenne pepper
1/2 cup beef stock
1 cans tomatoes -- 28 ozs.
1 cans tomato paste -- 8 oz.
4 cans red kidney beans -- 1 lb cans

Heat shortening in skillet and brown beef, discard fat. Combine all ingredients in removable liner, stirring well. Place liner in base. Cover and cook on low 8-10 hours; high 4-5 hours or auto 6-7 hours.

Crockpot Chili With 4 Kinds Of Beans

1-2 pounds browned ground beef
2 cans chili hot beans
2 cans dark red kidney beans, drained
2 cans pinto beans, drained
2 cans kidney beans, drained
2 cans rotel tomatoes
1 package chili seasoning

Put all ingredients in crock pot and cook on low all day (about 10 hours).

Crockpot Chinese Pepper Steak

4-6 servings 1-1 1/2 lbs boneless beef round steak
1 clove garlic minced
1/2 tsp. salt

1/4 tsp. pepper
1/4 cup soy sauce
1 tbsp. hoisin sauce
1 tsp. sugar
1 tomato, seeded, peeled & diced
2 red or green bell peppers cut into strips
3 tbsp. cornstarch
3 tbsp. water
1 cup fresh bean sprouts
4 green onions, finely chopped

Cooked rice trims fat from steak; slice into thin strips. Combine steak, garlic, salt, pepper, soy sauce, hoisin sauce and sugar in crock pot. Cover and cook on low about 4 hours. Turn control to high. Add tomato and bell peppers. Dissolve cornstarch with water in a small bowl and stir into steak mixture. Cover and cook on high 15-20 minutes or until thickened. Stir in bean sprouts, sprinkle with onions. Serve with rice.

Crockpot Chinese Pie

1 to 1 1/2 pounds ground beef
3/4 cup diced bell pepper (green and red if possible)
3/4 cup diced onion
1 package (dry) brown gravy
4 to 6 medium red or round white potatoes, diced (about 4 cups)
2 tablespoons butter, melted
1 (15 oz) can whole kernel corn, drained (or 2 cups frozen)
1 (15 oz) can creamed corn
Salt and pepper to taste

Brown ground beef with diced peppers and onion. Drain well. Place ground beef mixture in Crockpot. Toss diced potato with melted butter to coat and add to Crockpot; add whole kernel corn and creamed corn. Salt and pepper to taste. Cover and cook on low for 7 to 9 hours. Taste and adjust seasonings. Serves 4 to 6.

Crockpot Chocolate Apple Cake

6 tbsp butter
1/2 c sugar
1/2 c brown sugar
1 c unsweetened applesauce
1 tsp cinnamon
1 tsp pure vanilla extract

3 eggs
4 (1 oz) sq unsweetened chocolate, melted
1 1/2 c flour
2 tsp baking soda
1 tsp baking powder
Pinch of salt
1/3 c buttermilk
3/4 c semisweet chocolate chips
1/2 c chopped pecans
Confectioner's sugar

In a large bowl, beat together butter & sugars w/a mixer on high speed 1-2 minutes, or until fluffy. Beat in applesauce, cinnamon, vanilla & eggs until well mixed. Beat in melted chocolate until blended. Add flour, baking soda & powder, & salt. With mixer on low speed, beat in dry ingredients, adding buttermilk as you beat. Beat just until evenly mixed. By hand stir in chocolate chips & pecans. Scrape the batter into a well buttered 3 1/2 quart Crockpot & smooth top. Cover & cook on the high setting 2 1/4 to 2 1/2 hrs, or until a cake tester (toothpick) inserted in the center comes out clean. (Do not cook on the low heat setting for a longer time) remove lid & let cake stand in Crockpot until just barely warm. To unmold: run a sharp knife around the inside edges of the Crockpot & w/a large spatula carefully lift out the cake in one piece. Sprinkle with confectioner's sugar over top & cut into wedges to serve.

Crockpot Chocolate Apple Sauce Cake

6 tbsp butter
1 cup sugar
1 cup unsweetened applesauce
1 tsp cinnamon
1 tsp vanilla
3 eggs
4 (1 oz) squares unsweetened chocolate, melted
1 1/2 cups flour
2 tsp baking soda
1 tsp baking powder
Pinch of salt
1/3 cup buttermilk
3/4 cup semisweet chocolate chips
1/2 cup chopped walnuts powdered sugar

In a large bowl, beat together the butter and sugar w/a mixer on high speed 1-2 minutes, or until fluffy. Beat in the applesauce, cinnamon, vanilla and eggs until well mixed. Beat in the melted chocolate until blended. Add the flour, baking soda & powder, and salt. With the mixer on low speed, beat in the dry ingredients, adding the buttermilk as you beat. Beat just until evenly mixed. By hand, stir in chocolate chips and nuts. Scrape the batter into a well buttered 3 1/2 quart crock pot and smooth the top. Cover and cook on the high setting 2 1/4 to 2 1/2 hours, or until a cake tester inserted in the center comes out clean. (Do not cook on the low heat setting for a longer time) remove the lid and let the cake stand in the crock pot until just barely warm. To unmold, run a sharp knife around the inside edges of the crock and w/a large spatula, carefully lift out the cake in one piece. Sprinkle with powdered sugar over the top and cut into wedges to serve.

Crockpot Chocolate Clusters

2 pounds white almond bark
4 ounces bar German chocolate
1 pkg. semi-sweet chocolate chips (12 ounces)
24 ounces dry roasted peanuts

Put all ingredients in crock pot; cover and cook on high for 1 hour. Do not stir. Turn crock pot to low and stir every 15 minutes for 1 hour. Drop on waxed paper and let cool. Store in a tightly covered container.

Crockpot Chocolate Peanut Butter Cake

2 c. chocolate cake mix
1/2 c. water
1/3 c. creamy peanut butter
1/2 c. chopped nuts

Combine all ingredients in bowl mixing well. Beat about 2 minutes. Pour batter into greased and floured 2 pound coffee can. Place can in Crockpot. Cover top of can with 8 paper towels. Cover Crockpot and bake on high 2 to 3 hours.

Crockpot Chops Or Ribs

6 or 8 chops or ribs to fill crock pot
1/4 c chopped onion
1/2 c chopped celery
1 c catsup
1/2 c water
1/4 c lemon juice
2 tbsp brown sugar
3 tbsp Worcestershire sauce
2 tbsp vinegar

1 tbsp mustard
1/2 tsp salt
1/4 tsp pepper

Mix together & pour over meat in pot. Cook until tender.

Crockpot Chow Mien

4 oz. can mushrooms
1 1/2 lbs. cubed round steak
4 stocks celery
2 med. onions
1 c. hot water with 3 bouillon cubes
3 tbsp. soy sauce
2 tsp. Worcestershire sauce
1 lb. cans Chinese vegetables
2 tbsp. cornstarch and
2 tbsp. water

Cook 8 to 10 hours in Crockpot - 1 hour before serving add Chinese vegetables and cornstarch and water.

Crockpot Chunky Vegetable Clam Chowder

2 6 1/2 oz cans minced clams
2 c. peeled potatoes, cut into 1/2" cubes
1 c. finely chopped onion
1 c. chopped celery
1 tsp. sugar
1/4 tsp. salt
1/4 tsp. pepper
2 10 3/4 oz cans condensed cream of potato soup
2 c. water
1 c. nonfat dry milk powder
1/3 c. flour
1 c. cold water
4 slices bacon, crisp-cooked, drained, and crumbled
Paprika

Drain clams, reserving liquid. Cover clams; chill. in crock pot combine reserved clam liquid, potatoes, onion, celery, carrot, sugar, salt, and pepper. Stir in potato sour and 2 cups water. Cover; cook on low heat for 8 to 10 hours or on high heat for 4 to 5 hours. If using low heat setting, turn to high. In a medium bowl combine nonfat dry milk powder and flour. Gradually whisk in 1 c. cold water; stir into soup. Cover; cook on high 10 to 15 minutes or till thickened. Stir in clams. Cover; cook 5 minutes more. Ladle soup into bowls. Sprinkle each serving with crumbled bacon and paprika. Makes 6 to 8 servings.

Crockpot Clam Chowder I

4 cans of cream of potato soup
4 cans of New England clam chowder
2 cans minced clams with juice
1 onion, chopped and sautéed in 1 stick butter
1 quart half and half

Sauté onions in butter, then add all ingredients in Crockpot for 4 hours

Crockpot Clam Chowder II

4 (6 1/2 oz.) cans clams
1/2 lb. salt pork or bacon, diced
1 lg. onion, chopped
6 to 8 lg. potatoes, pared and cubed
3 c. water
3 1/2 tsp. salt
1/4 tsp. pepper
4 c. half and half cream or milk
3 to 4 tbsp. cornstarch

Cut clams into bite sized pieces if necessary. In skillet, sauté salt pork or bacon and onion until golden brown; drain. Put into crock pot with clams. Add all remaining ingredients, except milk. Cover; cook on high 3 to 4 hours or until potatoes are tender. During the last hour of cooking, combine 1 cup of milk with the cornstarch. Add that and the remaining milk and stir well; heat through. Serve in large bowls with crusty French bread.

Crockpot Cobbler

All you do is bake a batch of biscuits and let them cool. Chunk them up and put about half in the bottom of your Crockpot. Mix: 1/4 cup brown sugar 1/2 t. cinnamon 1/2 cup butter. Sprinkle some of that on top. Spread canned pie filling on top and repeat until you're out of ingredients. Bake on high for 2 hours.

Crockpot Coconut Thai Shrimp And Rice

2 (10 oz.) cans chicken broth
1 cup water
1 tsp. coriander
1/2 tsp. cumin
1 tsp salt
1/2 tsp cayenne pepper
Zest and juice of 2 limes (1/3 cup of juice)
7 cloves minced garlic
1 tbsp. minced fresh ginger
1 medium onion chopped
1 red bell pepper chopped
1 carrot peeled and shredded
1/4 cup flaked coconut
1/2 cup golden raisins
2 cups converted rice
1 lb. peeled and deveined jumbo cooking shrimp (thawed if frozen)
2 oz. fresh snow peas cut into strips toasted cocoanut for garnish (optional)

In a 5 qt cp, combine chicken broth, water, coriander, cumin, salt, cayenne pepper, lime zest, lime juice, garlic and ginger. Stir in onion, pepper, carrot, coconut, raisins and rice. Cover and cook on low 3 1/2 hours, or until rice is tender. Check after 3 hours and if liquid is absorbed, but rice is not tender, add 1 more cup water. When rice is tender, stir in shrimp and snow peas. Cook 30 minutes longer. Sprinkle with toasted coconut and serve.

Crockpot Cola Barbecue Pork Roast

1 pork roast
1 1/2 cup cola
1 bottle BBQ sauce

Cut all visible fat from roast, put in crock and cook 12 hrs remove meat from crock and drain all juice from crock. Shred meat and return to crock add 1 bottle bib sauce and cook 5-6 hrs more.

Crockpot Cola Ham

1/2 cup brown sugar
1 tsp dry mustard
1/4 cup cola (coca cola(r), Pepsi, etc)
3 to 4 pound pre-cooked ham

Combine brown sugar and mustard. Moisten with cola to make a smooth paste. Reserve remaining cola. Score the ham with shallow slashes in a diamond pattern. Rub ham with mixture. Place ham in Crockpot and add remaining cola. Cover and cook on high for 1 hour, then turn to low and cook for 6 to 7 hours. Serves 9 to 12.

Crockpot Coq Au Vin

12 sm white onions, peeled
4 lb roasting chicken, cut up
1/2 tsp salt
1/4 tsp black pepper
1/4 c brandy or cognac
2 ea cloves garlic, peeled and crushed
1/4 tsp ground thyme
1 ea bay leaf
1 1/2 c dry, strong red wine
5 tbsp all purpose flour
1 c chicken bouillon
3/4 lb fresh mushrooms, wiped and stemmed
1 tbsp butter or margarine
1/4 tsp salt
1 tbsp chopped fresh parsley

Place the onions in the crock pot. Remove the fat from the vent of the chicken and dice it. In a large skillet over medium heat, heat the fat until it is rendered. Discard the shriveled bits and sauté the chicken until well browned. Season with 1/2 tsp salt and the pepper. Warm the brandy in a ladle or a small saucepan; light it with match and pour it over the chicken. When the flame dies, lift the chicken into the crock pot and add the garlic, thyme, and bay leaf. Pour the wine into the hot skillet and scrape up the pan juices. Dissolve the flour in the bouillon, turn it into the skillet and bring to simmering, stirring briskly to prevent lumps. Turn into the crock pot. Cover and cook on low 7-9 hours. Before serving: about 10 minutes before serving, in a medium skillet, sauté the mushrooms in the butter over medium high heat. In about 5 minutes, they will be tender and the moisture will have evaporated from the skillet. Season with 1/4 tsp salt and add to the chicken casserole. If the sauce seems thin, simmer it in the mushroom skillet long enough to thicken to the consistency of heavy cream. Garnish the coq au vin with parsley before serving.

Crockpot Coq Au Vin

2-1/2 lb chicken cut up
1 clove garlic crushed
1 teaspoon salt

1/4 teaspoon pepper
1/2 teaspoon dried thyme
6 bacon slices, diced
2/3 cups sliced green onions
1 cup chicken broth
8 small white onions, peeled
1 cup burgundy wine
1/2 lb whole mushrooms
Chopped parsley
8 small new potatoes scrubbed

In large skillet, sauté deiced bacon and green onions until bacon is crisp. Remove and drain on paper towel. Add chicken pieces to skillet and brown well on all sides. Remove the chicken when it has browned and set aside. Put peeled onions, mushrooms, and garlic in Crockpot. Add browned chicken pieces, bacon and green onions, salt, pepper, thyme, pototales and chicken broth. Cover and cook on low 6 -8 hours (high 3-4). During the last hour add burgundy and cook on high. Garnish with chopped parsley.

Crockpot Coq Au Vin With Shiitake Mushrooms

2 tbs. olive oil
3 lb. chicken pieces, rinsed & patted dry
1/3 c finely chopped shallot
1/3 c finely chopped onion
2 carrots, quartered lengthwise & cut crosswise into 1/4" pieces (about 1/2 cup)
1/2 lb. pearl onions, blanched in boiling water for 3 minutes, drained, & peeled
1 bay leaf
3/4 tsp thyme, crumbled
2 tbs. cognac
1 c dry white wine
2 c chicken broth
1/4 lb. shiitake mushrooms, stems discarded & caps sliced thin
1/4 c cornstarch
Freshly ground nutmeg to taste

in a heavy kettle, heat the oil over moderately high heat until it is hot but not smoking and in it sauté the chicken pieces, seasoned with salt and pepper, in batches, turning them once, for 8 to 10 minutes, or until they are browned. Transfer the chicken pieces as they are browned to a plate and keep them warm, covered. Place the shallot, onions, carrots, pearl onions, bay leaf, and thyme in a Crockpot. Place the browned chicken on top of the vegetables. Combine the cognac, white wine and 1 3/4 cup of chicken broth and add to the cooker. Cover and cook on low for 5 hours or until chicken is tender. Turn control to high and add the mushrooms. Dissolve the cornstarch in the remaining 1/4 cup chicken stock. Stir into the mixture. Cover and cook for 20 minutes more, or until sauce is thickened, stirring once. Transfer the chicken to a plate, and keep warm. Discard the bay leaf, and season the sauce with freshly ground nutmeg and salt and pepper to taste. Serve warm. Serves 4 to 5.

Crockpot Corn Chowder I

6 slices bacon, diced
1/2 c. chopped onion
2 c. diced peeled potatoes
2 pkgs. (10 oz each) frozen whole-kernel corn, broken apart
1 cans (16 oz) cream-style corn
1 tbs. sugar
1 tsp. Worcestershire sauce
1 tsp. seasoned salt
1/4 tsp. pepper
1 c. water

In skillet, fry bacon until crisp; remove and reserve. Add onion and potatoes to bacon drippings and sauté for about 5 minutes; drain well. Combine all ingredients in crock pot; stir well. Cover and cook on low setting for 4 to 7 hours. Makes about 1 1/2 quarts.

Crockpot Corn Chowder II

3 16oz cans of corn, drained
2 large potatoes cut into 1" chunks
1 & 1/2 can chicken broth
1 large onion, diced
1 tsp. salt
Pepper
2 pints half and half
1/2 stick butter

Put everything except the dairy products in the Crockpot and cook on low for 7-8 hours. Remove to a blender, and puree. Return to Crockpot, add half & half and butter; stir. Cook on high for one hour. Stir and serve. Serves six.

Crockpot Corn Pudding

8 oz. cream cheese, softened
2 eggs, beaten
1/3 cup sugar

8 1/2 oz package corn bread mix
16 oz can cream style corn
2 1/3 cups frozen sweet corn
1 cup milk
2 tablespoons margarine, melted
1 tsp. salt
1/4 tsp nutmeg

Lightly grease crock pot. In a bowl, blend cream cheese, eggs and sugar. Add remaining ingredients and mix well. Pour into crock pot. Cover and cook on high 3 to 4 hours. Serves 10 to 12

Crockpot Corned Beef And Cabbage

4 1/2 lb. corned beef brisket
2 med onions, quartered
1 cabbage head cut in small wedges
1/2 tsp. pepper
3 tbsp. vinegar
3 tbsp. sugar
2 c. water

Combine ingredients in removable liner with cabbage on top. Cut meat to fit, if necessary. Place liner in base. Cover and cook on low 10-12 hours, high 6-7 hours, or auto 6-8 hours.

Crockpot Corned Beef And Cabbage

3 lb uncooked corned beef brisket (in pouch with pickling juice is okay)
2 carrots, chopped into 2" pieces
5 small red potatoes, halved
1 onion, quartered
1 small turnip, chopped into 2" pieces
3/4 cup malt vinegar
1/2 bottle (6 oz) Irish stout
1 tsp mustard seed
1 tsp coriander seed
1 tsp black peppercorns (whole)
1 tsp dill seed
1 tsp allspice (whole)
1 bay leaf
1 small (2 lb) head cabbage, cut into wedges

In a large (6.5 qt) crock-pot, place the carrots, spuds, onion and turnip in bottom. Add the liquids. Spice rubs the brisket. Place on top. Cover and cook on low for 8 hours. Add cabbage wedges. Cook an additional 3 hours on low. Serve with coarse grain mustard and horseradish sauce.

Horseradish sauce:
1/2 pint whipping cream
3 tbsp prepared horseradish
Whip cream until it peaks, then fold in horseradish.

Crockpot Corned Beef Hash I

1 can of corned beef (or 2 cups of cooked corned beef)
1 med onion shredded
2 med. celery sticks chopped
5 fair sized potatoes chopped
2 tbsp. butter
1 diced green pepper
Garlic to your taste
1 cup mushrooms
1 tbsp Worchestshire sauce
A dash or two of Italian seasoning
Salt and pepper to taste
2- 10 oz cans of chicken broth

Grind up or chop your corned beef and toss it in the crock pot with all the other ingredients in the list above. Cook in your crock pot on low for 8 hours. When the potatoes are well cooked mash them in the pot and add a little water if need be. Then serve it with warm bread and salad!

Crockpot Corned Beef Hash II

1 tin of corned beef hash
3 big potatoes
3 ribs of celery chopped
1 large onion chopped
2 big cloves of garlic
Salt and pepper to taste
A dash or so of basil
2 tins of chicken broth

Fry the garlic, celery, onion, and salt and pepper in a tbsp of garlic till veggies are tender. Then toss everything in the crock pot and turn on low for about 5-6 hours. Serve with lots of warm bread and butter.

Crockpot Corny Ham And Potato Scallop

5 potatoes, peeled and cubed
1 1/2 cups cubed cooked ham
1 (15 ounce) can whole kernel corn, drained
1/4 cup chopped green bell pepper
2 teaspoons instant minced onion
1 (11 ounce) can condensed cheddar cheese soup
1/2 cup milk
3 tablespoons all-purpose flour

In a 3 1/2 to 4 quart crock pot, combine potatoes, ham, corn, green pepper and onion; mix well. In a small bowl, combine soup, milk and flour; beat with wire whisk until smooth. Pour soup mixture over potato mixture and stir gently to mix. Cover and cook on low setting for about 8 hours or until potatoes are tender.

Crockpot Costa Rican Beef & Vegetable Soup With Yellow Rice

2 lb lean, boneless beef chuck in 1 1/2 inch cubes
1 lg onion, thinly sliced
1 c celery, thinly sliced
3 cloves garlic, minced
1 dry bay leaf
1 lg red bell pepper, seeded and cut into thin, bite-size strips
1 1/2 c water
2 cans (about 14 1/2 oz.) beef broth
1 lg ear corn, cut into 3/4 inch thick slices
4 c coarsely shredded cabbage
1/3 c lightly packed cilantro leaves
Salt and pepper
Rice

The soup:
Arrange beef cubes slightly apart in a single layer in a shallow baking pan. Bake in a 500 oven until well browned (about 20 minutes). Meanwhile, in a 3 1/2 quart or larger Crockpot, combine onion, celery, garlic, bay leaf and bell pepper. Transfer browned beef to Crockpot. Pour a little of the water into baking pan, stirring to dissolve drippings and pour into Crockpot. Add broth and remaining water. Cover and cook on low about 8 hours. About 15

minutes before beef is done, prepare yellow rice. While rice is cooking, increase cooker setting to high; add corn. Cover; cook for 5 minutes. Add cabbage; cover and cook until cabbage is bright green, 8 to 10 more minutes. Stir in cilantro; season with salt and pepper. Ladle soup into wide, shallow bowls; add a scoop of rice to each.

The rice:
1 tablespoon salad oil
1 small onion, finely chopped
1 cup long-grain white rice
1/4 teaspoon ground turmeric
1 3/4 cups water

Heat oil in 2-quart pan over medium heat. Add the onion; cook, stirring until onion is soft but not browned, (3 to 5 minutes). Stir in the rice and turmeric; cook, stirring occasionally, for about 1 minute. Pour in the water and reduce heat to low and cook until rice is tender, about 20 minutes.

Crockpot Country Chicken Stew With Basil Dumplings

12 small white onions water
1 pound boneless skinless chicken thighs
1 pound boneless skinless chicken breasts halves
1/2 tablespoon chopped fresh basil leaves (or 1/2 teaspoon dried, crumbled)
Salt and pepper to taste
1 large red bell pepper cut into 1" squares
4 cloves garlic - thinly sliced
2 cups canned chicken broth
1/3 cup dry white wine
2 tablespoons all purpose flour
2 tablespoon butter - room temperature
1 pound fresh asparagus - cut into 1-1/2" lengths

Dumplings:
1 cup buttermilk and baking mix
1/3 cup whole milk
1/4 cup chopped fresh basil leaves (or 1 tablespoon dried, crumbled)

Using a sharp knife, make a small x in the root end of each onion. Bring a saucepan of water to boil. Add the onions, lower the heat, and simmer for 5 minutes. Drain and rinse under running cold water. Slip skins off onions. Rinse chicken and pat dry. Quarter the thighs and chicken breast halves. Stir in basil and season with salt and pepper. Put chicken pieces in a 3-

1/2 quart or larger crockery slow-cooker. Top with onions, bell peppers, and garlic. Pour in stock, and wine. Do not stir. Cover and cook on low for 6 - 8 hours or high for 2 - 2-1/2 hours. Stir the stew. If cooking on low, change setting to high. In a small bowl, blend together the flour and butter. Stir into slow-cooker. Cook, stirring until sauce begins to thicken, about 5 minutes. Stir in asparagus. In medium bowl, combine dumpling ingredients until evenly moistened. Drop by tablespoons onto hot stew in 6 small rounds. Cover and cook for another 25 to 30 minutes, until dumplings are cooked through. Serve immediately!

Crockpot Country Style Ribs And Kraut

12 oz sauerkraut
Brown sugar to taste
1-2 lbs country style ribs

Place the ribs in a Crockpot. Sweeten the sauerkraut to taste with the brown sugar. Cook them all day while at work and come home to tender and delicious ribs and kraut. Mash a potato and dinner is ready!

Crockpot Cranapple Sauce

10-12 medium apples
1-2 cups cranberry juice
Lemon juice -- use 1/4 to 1/2 lemon
2 tbs sugar -- or up to 1/4 cup if you want it sweet
1/4 to 1/2 cup dried cranberries or "craisins" (sweetened dried cranberries)

Wash the apples and chop them up without peeling. Squeeze lemon juice over them as you cut them. Put apples in Crockpot with cranberry juice -- use 1 cup if you want the applesauce thick, more if you want it thin. Stir in sugar to suit your taste. Let apples stew on low for 6-8 hours. About an hour or two before serving, stir in cranberries or craisins.

Crockpot Cranberries

1 pkg. fresh cranberries
2 c. sugar
1/4 c. water

Combine cranberries with sugar and water in crock pot. Cover and cook on high 2 to3 hours until some pop. Serve with turkey or chicken.

Crockpot Cranberry Chicken

1 small onion, thinly sliced

1 cup fresh or frozen (unthawed) cranberries
12 skinless, boneless chicken thighs (about 2 1/4 lbs. total)
1/4 cup catsup
2 tablespoons firmly packed brown sugar
1 teaspoon dry mustard
2 teaspoons cider vinegar
1 1/2 tablespoons cornstarch blended w/2 tablespoons cold water
Salt

In a 3-quart or larger electric crock pot, combine onion, cranberries. Arrange chicken on top. In small bowl, mix catsup, sugar, mustard and vinegar and pour over chicken. Cover. Cook at low setting until chicken is very tender when pierced (6 1/2 to 7 1/2 hours). Lift out chicken when done; blend cornstarch mixture into cooking liquid. Increase cooker heat setting to high; cover and cook, stirring 2 or 3 times until sauce thickens (10 to 15 more minutes). Season to taste with salt; pour over chicken. Makes 6 servings.

Crockpot Cranberry Pork

1 (16 ounce) can cranberry sauce
1/3 cup French salad dressing
1 onion, sliced
3 pounds pork roast

In a medium bowl, combine the cranberry sauce, salad dressing and onions. Place pork in a crock pot and pour the sauce over the pork. Cook on high setting for 4hours or on low setting for 8 hours. Pork is done when its internal temperature has reached 160°f (70°c).

Crockpot Cranberry Pork Roast

4 medium potatoes, peeled and cut into 1" chunks
One 3-pound boneless center-cut pork loin roast, rolled and tied
1 cans (16 ounces) whole-berry cranberry sauce
1 can (5.5 ounces) apricot nectar
1 medium onion, coarsely chopped
1/2 cup coarsely chopped dried apricots
1/2 cup sugar
1 teaspoon dry mustard
1/4 teaspoon crushed red pepper

Place the potatoes in a 3 1/2-quart (or larger) crock pot, and then place the roast over the potatoes. In a large bowl, combine the remaining ingredients; mix well and pour over the roast. Cover and cook on the low setting for 5 to 6 hours. Remove the roast to a cutting board and thinly slice. Serve with the potatoes and sauce.

Crockpot Crazy Standing Up Pork Chops

4 loin pork chops -- lean
2 med onions -- sliced
1 tsp butter
Salt & pepper -- to taste
Spices of your choice

Stand chops in Crockpot, thin side down. Sprinkle with salt, pepper and spices of your choice. Cover with the onion slices, which have been separated into rings. Place butter on top, and cook on low heat for 6 to 8 hours, or until chops are tender and onions are done. The result is moist, tender chops with a deep brown color as if broiled in the oven.

Crockpot Cream Cheese Chicken

1 frying chicken -- cut up
2 tablespoons melted butter or margarine
Salt & pepper -- to taste
2 tablespoons dry Italian salad dressing
1 can condensed mushroom soup
6 ounces cream cheese; -- cut in 1" cubes
1/2 cup sauterne wine or sherry
1 tablespoon onion -- minced

Brush chicken with butter and sprinkle with salt and pepper. Place in a Crockpot and sprinkle dry mix over all. Cover and cook on low for 6 - 7 hours. About 45 minutes before done, mix soup, cream cheese, wine, and onion in a small saucepan. Cook until smooth. Pour over the chicken and cover and cook another 45 minutes. Serve with sauce.

Crockpot Cream Of Sweet Potato Soup

3 sweet potatoes, peeled and sliced
2 c chicken bouillon
1 tsp sugar
1/8 tsp each ground cloves and nutmeg
Salt to taste
1 1/2 c light cream, half-and-half, or milk

Put sweet potatoes and bouillon in cooker. Cover and cook on high 2 to 3 hours or until potatoes are tender. Force potatoes and liquid through food mill or puree in blender. Put back in cooker with remaining ingredients. Cover and cook on high 1 to2 hours. Serve hot or chilled with a dollop of sour cream if desired. Makes about 1 quart.

Crockpot Creamy Chicken Dinner

4 boneless/skinless chicken breasts seasoned with garlic powder, onion powder and season salt
1 large can cream of chicken soup
2 cans cream of mushroom soup
3/4 c frozen cut carrots
3/4 c frozen green beans

Dump it all in the Crockpot and cook it about 7 hours on low. Add 2 cups of minute rice to it the last 5 minutes before dinner.

Crockpot Creamy Hash Browns

1 2-lb pkg frozen cubed hash brown potatoes
8 oz shredded or cubed Velveeta
16 oz sour cream
1 can cream of celery soup
1 can cream of chicken soup
1 lb bacon, cooked & crumbled
1 lg onion, chopped
1/4 c butter or margarine, melted
1/4 tsp pepper

Place potatoes in an ungreased Crockpot. In a bowl, combine the remaining ingredients. Pour over potatoes and mix well. Cover and cook on low for 4-5 hours (until potatoes are tender and heated through). You can serve it with biscuits and fruit salad.

Crockpot Creamy Orange Cheesecake

Crust:
3/4 cup cookie or graham cracker crumbs
2 tablespoons sugar
3 tablespoons melted butter

Filling:
16 ounces cream cheese (light)
2/3 cup sugar
2 eggs
1 egg yolk

1/4 cup frozen orange juice concentrate, thawed
1 teaspoon orange or lemon zest or dried grated rind
1 tablespoon flour
1/2 teaspoon vanilla

Combine crumbs with sugar; mix in melted butter until well moistened. Pat into a 7-inch spring form pan. In a medium bowl, cream together the cream cheese and sugar. Add eggs and yolk and beat for about 3 minutes on medium with a hand-held electric mixer. Beat in orange juice, zest, flour, and vanilla. Beat for another 2 minutes. Pour batter into prepared crust; place on a rack or aluminum foil ring in the crockery cooker (so it doesn't rest on the bottom of the pot). Cover and cook on high for 2 1/2 to 3 hours. Turn off and leave for 1 to 2 hours, until cool enough to remove. Cool completely and remove the sides of the pan. Chill before serving, and store leftovers in the refrigerator.

Crockpot Creamy Red Potatoes

2 lbs small red potatoes, quartered
2 (8 oz) pkgs. cream cheese, softened
1 can cream of potato soup, undiluted
1 envelope ranch salad dressing mix

Place potatoes in Crockpot. In a small bowl, beat cream cheese, soup and salad dressing, mix. Stir into potatoes. Cover and cook on low for 8 hours or until potatoes are tender. Also add about a tablespoon of milk.

Crockpot Creamy Spinach N0odle Casserole

8 ounces dry spinach noodles
2 tbsp. vegetable oil
1 1/2 cups sour cream
1/3 cup all-purpose flour
1 1/2 cups cottage cheese
4 green onions, minced
2 tsp. Worcestershire sauce
1 dash hot pepper sauce
2 tsp. garlic salt

Cook noodles in a pot of salted, boiling water until just tender. Drain and rinse with cold water. Toss with vegetable oil. Combine sour cream and flour in a large bowl, mixing well. Stir in cottage cheese, green onions, Worcestershire sauce, hot pepper sauce and garlic salt. Fold noodles into mixture until well combined. Generously grease the inside of a crock pot and pour in noodle mixture. Cover and cook on high for 1 1/2 to 2 hours.

Crockpot Creole Black Beans

1 to 2 pounds smoked sausage, cut into 1" slices
3 15 oz cans black beans, drained
1 1/2 cups onions -- chopped
1 1/2 cups green pepper, chopped
1 1/2 cups celery, chopped
3 cloves garlic, minced
2 teaspoons leaf thyme
1 1/2 teaspoons leaf oregano
1 1/2 teaspoons white pepper
1/4 teaspoon black pepper
1/4 teaspoon cayenne pepper
1 chicken bouillon cube
5 bay leaves
1 cans 8-oz. tomato sauce
1 cup water
Hot boiled rice

Brown sausage in a skillet over med. heat. Drain fat and transfer to Crockpot. Combine remaining ingredients in Crockpot. Cover and cook on low 8 hrs. Or on high 4 hrs. Remove bay leaves. Serve over cooked rice. Serves 6 to 8.

Crockpot Creole Chicken

8 chicken thighs
1 can diced tomatoes
1 cans tomato paste
1 chopped bell pepper
1 chopped onion chopped ham
Diced sausage
Tabasco sauce to taste

Throw it all in the crock and cook on low 4-5 hours.

Crockpot Crystal's Leftover Pork Roast Casserole

1 package cooked noodles
1 package beans
Beef bouillon
1 package long grain and wild rice
3 potatoes cut into 1" cubes
Leftover pork from your roast

Salt and pepper to taste

Fill your Crockpot a little more than half way with water, and then flavor it with the beef bullion to taste. Add the sliced up potatoes, beans and rice. Cook until potatoes and rice are done, most of the day on low or half of the day on high. Add the pork and let that cook while you boil the noodles. Add the noodles to the pot when they're done. Let cook for 5 to 10 more minutes and serve.

Crockpot Custard

3 eggs, lightly beaten
1/3 cup sugar
1 teaspoon vanilla
2 cups milk
1/4 teaspoon ground nutmeg

In a mixing bowl combine eggs, sugar, vanilla and milk; mix well. Pour into a lightly buttered 1-or 1 1/2-quart baking dish or soufflé which will fit in the crock pot, and sprinkle with the nutmeg. Place a rack or ring of aluminum foil in the crock pot, then add 1 1/2 to 2 cups of hot water to the pot. Cover the baking dish with aluminum foil and place on the rack in the crock pot. Cover and cook on high for 2 1/2 to 3 hours, or until set. Serves 4 to 6.

Crockpot Deer Chili

3 1/2 lbs. deer chuck roast
1 (1 lb.) can tomatoes
1/2 c. water
1 c. chopped onion
1 clove garlic
1 cans chili beans
2 tsp. chili powder
1 can chili beef soup
1/2 c. diced green pepper
Rice

Cut meat into 1" strips. Roll in flour. Brown in skillet. Put in crock pot. Add tomatoes, water, onion, chili powder, soup, chili beans, garlic and green pepper. Set on low to low-medium heat setting for about 6 hours. Serve with rice.

Crockpot Dressing

1 (8 inch) pan cornbread
8 slices dry white bread
4 eggs
2 c. chicken broth
2 cans cream of chicken soup
1 tsp. sage
1/2 tsp. black pepper
Celery to taste
1 med. onion
2 tbsp. butter

Mix ingredients except butter. Place in crock pot. Dot butter on top. Cook 2 hours on high then 4 hours on low.

Crockpot Fruit Dessert

3 grapefruit, peeled sectioned
1 can (11 oz) mandarin orange, sections, drained
1 cans (16 oz) fruit cocktail, well drained
1 cans (20 oz) pineapple chunks, well drained
1 can (16 oz) sliced peaches, well drained
3 bananas, sliced
1 tablespoon lemon juice
1 can (21 oz) cherry pie filling

Place all ingredients in cooker. Toss gently. Cover and cook on low about 4 hours. Makes about 2 quarts.

Crockpot Hamburger Casserole

2 lbs. browned ground beef
3 carrots, peeled and sliced
2 onions, sliced
4 potatoes, peeled and sliced
1 can peas, drained
2 stalks celery, diced
1 can cream of chicken soup
1 can water

Place potatoes in bottom of Crockpot, top with carrots and other vegetables. Place ground beef on top. Combine soup and water and pour over ground beef. Cover and cook on low for 6 to 8 hours.

Crockpot Hamburger-Sausage Dip

1 pound ground chuck
1 cup picante sauce
1 can cream of mushroom soup
2 pound Velveeta cheese...cut into pieces
1 pound pork sausage
1 teaspoon garlic powder
1 cans rotel tomatoes
3/4 teaspoon oregano

Combine picante sauce, garlic powder, soup, tomatoes, oregano and cheese in crock pot. Brown ground chuck and sausage until it is done. Drain very well and place in crock pot. Cook on low until cheese is melted. Serve with your favorite chips.

Crockpot Hot Dip

1 pound Italian sausage - hot
1 pounds Velveeta - Mexican type - hot
1 can rotel tomatoes (drained)
1 jar pace picante sauce - hot
1 jalapeno pepper - finely diced

Brown sausage and drain along with jalapeno pepper. Add to crock pot with other ingredients and simmer on low for 1 hour or more until melted and blended. Serve with tortilla strips or chips, large Fritos corn chips, or even lightly toasted and cubed sourdough bread.

Crockpot Jambalaya

1 pound chicken breasts, boneless, cut in 1" cubes
1 pound smoked sausage, sliced
1 pound shrimp, cooked
28 ounces crushed tomatoes
1 med onion, chopped
1 green pepper, chopped
1 cup chicken broth
1/2 cup white wine
2 teaspoons oregano
2 teaspoons parsley

2 teaspoons Cajun seasoning
1 teaspoon cayenne pepper
2 cups rice, cooked

Cut chicken and slice sausage. Chop onion and green pepper. Put all in crock pot. Add remaining ingredients, except shrimp and rice. Cook in crock pot on low for 6-8 hours. 30 minutes before eating, add cooked shrimp and cooked rice; allow to heat. Can be cooked on high for 3-4 hours instead.

Crockpot Lasagna

1 pkg. pepperoni slices
1 lb. hamburger
1 onion, diced
1 green pepper, diced
1 can mushrooms
1 pkg. kluski noodles
1 lg. jar pizza sauce
1 lg. jar spaghetti sauce
1 pkg. each shredded Colby & mozzarella cheese

Cook together hamburger, onion, green pepper and mushrooms. Layer this with the rest of the ingredients in the crock pot. Cook on high for 2 to 3 hours.

Crockpot Little Smokies

2 packages cocktail wieners
1 medium bottle chili sauce
1 medium jar grape jelly

Combine in crock pot and cook on low 6 to 8 hours.

Crockpot Macaroni And Cheese

1 (16 oz.) pkg. macaroni, cooked & drained
1 tbsp. salad oil
1 (13 oz.) can evaporated milk
1 1/2 c. milk
1 tsp. salt
3 c. shredded sharp cheddar cheese
1/2 c. melted butter

Lightly grease crock pot. Toss macaroni and oil. Add all remaining ingredients. Stir, cover and cook on low 3 to 4 hours, stirring occasionally.

Crockpot Meatballs

2 pounds hamburger
1 cup breadcrumbs
1 each egg
Grated parmesan cheese
Parsley and oregano
Onion and garlic powder
Milk
1 cans beer
1 bottle ketchup, regular size

Mix hamburger, breadcrumbs, egg, seasonings and milk together. Make small meatballs. Mix ketchup and beer in the crock pot and start to heat. You can put the raw meatballs into the sauce and simmer for several hours.

Crockpot Potato Soup

6-8 potatoes, chunked
2 med. carrots, cubed
2 stalks celery, cubed
1 med. onion, chopped
1 tbsp. parsley flakes
5 c. water
Salt and pepper to taste

Cook in crock pot on low for 8 hours or until vegetables are done. One hour before serving, add one can of evaporated milk.

Crockpot Roast

2 1/2 lb. chuck roast
2 packets dry Italian dressing mix or ranch dressing mix
1 cup water

Place beef in crock pot, sprinkle seasonings over meat, pour water over all. Cook on low 6-8 hours or until meat shreds easily.

Crockpot Scrabble

2 cups wheat chex
2 cups corn chex
2 cups rice chex
3 cups thin pretzel sticks
1 13 ounce can or jar of salted peanuts or asst. mixed nuts
1 teaspoon garlic salt
1 teaspoon celery salt
1/2 teaspoon seasoned salt
2 tablespoons grated parmesan cheese
1/3 cup melted butter
1/3 cup Worcestershire sauce

In large (double) paper bag, mix together pretzels, cereals, and nuts along with the garlic salt, celery salt, seasoned salt, and grated cheese. Empty bag into large mixing bowl and sprinkle the melted butter and Worcestershire sauce over all mixing gently with your hands. Empty bowl into crock pot and cook on low for 3 or 4 hours. Tear open paper bags you used to originally mix the scrabble and spread them out onto a counter. Spread heated crock pot scrabble onto torn open bags and let dry for a minimum of one hour letting the paper absorb any excess moisture. Store in airtight containers. Keeps for several weeks without going stale.

Crockpot Spaghetti Sauce

4 tbsp. cooking oil
1 sm. onion, finely chopped
1 (15 1/2 oz.) can tomato sauce
1 1/2 c. water
1/2 tsp. pepper
1/2 tsp. red pepper, optional
1 lb. ground beef
1 (29 oz.) can tomato puree
1 (6 oz.) can tomato paste
1 tsp. salt
1/2 tsp. oregano
2 lbs. sausage (Italian links or country style)

Brown ground beef in 2 tablespoon hot oil in frying pan. When almost browned, add onion and continue browning until onion is tender. Pour meat and onion into 3 1/2 quart Crockpot. Add puree, sauce, paste, water, salt, pepper and oregano and set dial on low setting. Cut 2 lbs. sausage into pieces and brown in remaining 2 tablespoons oil. When brown, place sausages in sauce in Crockpot. Continue cooking for 12 hours.

Crockpot Spicy Dip

2 lb. Velveeta cheese
2 lb. hamburger, cooked and drained
1 lg. jar old El Paso taco sauce (or rotel tomatoes)
1 lg. onion, chopped fine

Mix all together in crock pot where cheese will melt and all will remaining warm.

Crockpot Split Pea Soup

1 (16 oz.) pkg. dried green split peas, rinsed
1 hambone, or 2 meaty ham hocks, or 2 c. diced ham
3 carrots, peeled & sliced
1 med. onion, chopped
2 stalks of celery plus leaves, chopped
1 or 2 cloves of garlic, minced
1 bay leaf
1/4 c. fresh parsley, chopped (optional)
1 tbsp. seasoned salt (or to taste)
1/2 tsp. fresh pepper
1 1/2 qts. Hot water

Layer ingredients in crock pot, pour in water. Do not stir. Cover and cook on high 4 to 5 hours or on low 8 to 10 hours until peas are very soft and ham falls off bone. Remove bones and bay leaf. Serve garnished with croutons.

Crockpot Swiss Steak

1 1/2 - 2 lb. round steak
2 tbsp. flour
1 sliced green pepper
1 tsp. salt
1/8 tsp. pepper
2 tbsp. salad oil
1 lg. onion, sliced
1 (16 oz.) can tomatoes, cut up
1 stalk celery, thinly sliced
1 tbsp. thick bottled steak sauce

Cut steak into serving size pieces. Coat with flour, salt and pepper. In large skillet or slow cooking pot with browning unit, brown meat in oil. Pour off excessive fat. In slow cooking pot, combine meat with tomatoes, onion, green pepper and steak sauce. Cover pot and cook on low for 6 to 8 hours or until tender. Thicken juices with additional flour, dissolved in a small amount of water, if desired. Makes 5 or 6 servings. Serve with mashed potatoes.

Crockpot Tenderloin Tips

1 lb. tenderloin tips
1 can mushroom soup
1 pkg. onion soup mix
1/4 c. water

Combine ingredients in crock pot. Cook 8 hours. Serve over noodles.

Crockpot Turkey Meatballs

1 1/2 cups barbecue sauce
10 ounces apple jelly
2 tablespoons tapioca
1 tablespoon vinegar
1 egg, beaten
1/4 cup seasoned bread crumbs, fine
2 tablespoons milk
1/4 teaspoon garlic powder
1/4 teaspoon salt
1/4 teaspoon onion powder
1 pound ground turkey
Non-stick vegetable spray

In 3 1/2 or 4 quart crockery cooker: stir together barbecue sauce, jelly, tapioca (if used), and vinegar. Cover; cook on high-heat setting while preparing meatballs. For meatballs, in large bowl combine egg, bread crumbs, milk, garlic powder, salt, and onion powder. Add ground turkey and mix well. Shape into 1/2 to 3/4-inch meatballs. Spray a 12-inch non-stick skillet; add meatballs and brown on all sides over med. heat. Drain meatballs. Add meatballs to crock pot; stir gently. Cover; cook on high heat setting for 1 1/2 to 2 hours. Makes 30 meatballs. Note: for 5 or 6-quart crock pot, double all ingredients. Prepare as above. Makes 60 meatballs.

Crockpot Turkey Sandwiches

6 c. diced turkey
3 c. diced cheese
1 can cream of mushroom soup
1 can cream of chicken soup
1 onion, chopped
1/2 c. miracle whip

Mix all of above and put in crock pot for 3-4 hours. Stir occasionally. Add liquid, if needed. Serve with buns.

Curried Fruit Bake

1 package prunes, (16 oz) pitted
1 package dried apricots (11 oz)
2 cans pineapple chunks (13 1/2 oz)
Drained
1 can peaches; sliced (1 lb 13 oz)
1 cup brown sugar
1/2 teaspoon curry powder
14 ounces ginger ale

Combine all ingredients in removable liner. Place in base. Cover and cook on low 4-5 hours or auto 3 hours.

Duck Gumbo

2 wild ducks, parboiled for 10 minutes
2 stalks celery, diced
1/2 bell pepper, diced
2 med. onions, diced
1/2 lb. smoked link sausage
Worcestershire sauce
Flour
Garlic salt
Oil
Salt and pepper

Make a dark roux with the oil, flour and seasonings. Add 2 cups water to make gravy. Allow to simmer while preparing next step. Chop vegetables and place in bottom of crock pot. Place ducks on top of vegetables. Pour gravy over ducks and vegetables. Turn crock pot on low and cook at least 8 hours. Two hours before serving, de-bone ducks, return meat to crock pot, slice sausage and add to gumbo. Serve over rice, adding Tabasco, Worcestershire or any other flavoring to taste.

Dumpling Soup

1 lb. lean steak, cut into 1" cubes
1 pkg. onion soup mix
6 c. water (hot)
2 carrots, peeled & shredded
1 stalk finely chopped celery
1 tomato, peeled & chopped
1 c. pkg. biscuit mix
6 tbsp. milk
1 tbsp. finely chopped parsley

With pot on low, sprinkle steak with dry onion soup mix. Pour hot water over steak. Stir in carrots, celery and tomato. Cover and cook on low 4-6 hours or until meat is tender. Turn pot control to high. In separate small bowl, combine biscuit mix with parsley. Stir in milk with fork until mixture is moistened. Drop dumpling mixture into crock pot with a teaspoon. Cover and cook on high for about 30 minutes.
5-6 servings.

Easy Chocolate Clusters

2 pounds white candy coating, broken into small pieces
2 cups semisweet chocolate chips
1 pkg. (4 oz) German sweet chocolate
1 jar (24 oz) dry roasted peanuts

In a crock pot, combine candy coating, German chocolate and chocolate chips. Cover and cook on high for 1 hour, then reduce heat to low. Cover and cook 1 hour longer or until melted, stirring every 15 minutes. Add peanuts and mix well. Drop by teaspoonfuls onto waxed paper; let stand until set. Store at room temperature. Makes about 3 1/2 dozen.

Easy Swiss Steak

2 to 2 1/2 lbs. round steak
1 pkg. onion soup mix
1/4 c. water
1 (10 oz.) can cream of mushroom soup

Cut steak into 5 to 6 serving size pieces. Place in crock pot. Add dry onion soup mix, water and soup. Cover and cook for 6 to 8 hours. Excellent with mashed potatoes. If you like lots of gravy use 2 packages soup mix and 2 cans of soup.

Eggplant Parmigiana

4 large eggplants
2 eggs
1/3 cup water
3 tablespoons flour
1/3 cup seasoned bread crumbs
1/2 cup parmesan cheese
1 cans marinara sauce, 2 lb
1 pound mozzarella cheese, sliced
Olive oil, extra virgin

Pare eggplant and cut in 1/2 inch slices; place in bowl in layers and sprinkle each layer with salt and let stand 30 minutes to drain excess water; dry on paper towels. Mix egg with water and flour. Dip eggplant slices in mixture, drain slightly. Sauté a few slices at a time quickly in hot olive oil. Combine seasoned bread crumbs with the parmesan cheese. In removable liner, layer one-fourth of the eggplant, top with one-fourth of the crumbs, one-fourth of the marinara sauce and one-fourth of the mozzarella cheese. Repeat three times to make four layers of eggplant, crumbs, sauce and mozzarella cheese. Place liner in base. Cover and cook on low 4-5 hours or auto 3 hours.

Enchilada Casserole

2 lbs. lean ground beef
1 med. onion, chopped
1 clove garlic, minced
1 (15 oz.) can tomato sauce
2 to 3 tbsp. chili powder or to taste
Salt & pepper
8 flour tortillas
1 can cream of chicken soup
3/4 c. milk2 c.
Cheddar cheese, shredded

Brown beef, onion and garlic. Add tomato sauce and chili powder; salt and pepper. Heat thoroughly. Spray crock pot with pam. Line with 2 tortillas. Cover with 1/3 of meat mixture and cheese. Layer 2 more times beginning with tortillas, meat mixture and cheese.

Top with 2 more tortillas. Combine soup and milk. Pour over top tortillas. Sprinkle with remaining cheese. Cook on low for 4 to 5 hours.

Favorite Crockpot Chili

2 lbs. coarsely ground beef chuck
2 (16 oz.) cans red kidney beans, drained
2 (14 1/2 oz.) cans tomatoes, drained
2 med. onions, coarsely chopped
1 green pepper, seeded and coarsely chopped
2 cloves garlic, peel and crushed
2-3 tbsp. chili powder
1 tsp. black pepper
1 tsp. cumin
Salt and pepper to taste

In a large, preferably non-stick, saucepan brown the chuck and drain off the fat. Put the ground beef and other ingredients in a 3 1/2 to 4 quart crock pot. If you have a small crock pot, cut the recipe in half. Stir well. Cover and cook on low for 10-12 hours. Makes 12 cups of chili

Fiesta Chicken

2 tablespoons oil
3 pounds boneless, skinless chicken breasts cut into 1-inch pieces
1 medium onion, chopped
1 teaspoon oregano
1 small jalapeno pepper, finely chopped
3 cloves garlic, minced
1 can (14 1/2 ounce) Mexican style diced tomatoes
1/4 teaspoon ground cumin

Heat oil in skillet. Cook chicken pieces until browned. Remove and drain. Place onion, green bell pepper, garlic and jalapeno pepper in skillet and sauté until slightly cooked. Add all ingredients to Crockpot and stir to combine. Cover; cook on low 8 hours (high 4 hours). Serve on flour tortillas.

Franks In Spicy Tomato Sauce

1 cup ketchup
1/2 cup firmly packed brown sugar
1 tablespoon red wine vinegar
2 teaspoons soy sauce

1 teaspoon Dijon mustard
1 clove garlic, minced
1 pound beef or chicken frankfurters, cut into 1" pieces

Place ketchup, brown sugar, vinegar, soy sauce, mustard, and garlic in the crockery pot. Cover and cook on high until blended. Stir occasionally. Add frankfurters and stir to coat. Cook until thoroughly blended. Serve with toothpicks or wooden skewers to spear franks.

Fresh Apple Coffeecake

2 cups biscuit mix
2/3 cup applesauce
1/4 cup milk
2 tablespoons sugar
2 tablespoons butter or margarine, softened or melted
2 apples, peeled, cored and diced
1 teaspoon cinnamon
1 teaspoon vanilla
1 egg, lightly beaten

Streusel
1/4 cup biscuit mix
1/4 cup brown sugar
2 tablespoons firm butter or margarine
1 teaspoon cinnamon
1/4 cup chopped nuts, if desired

Combine first 9 ingredients. Spread in a lightly greased 3 1/2 quart crock pot (or spread in a lightly greased baking dish which fits in a larger sized crock pot). Combine streusel ingredients with a fork or pastry blender; sprinkle over the batter. Cover and cook on high for about 2 1/2 hours, until a toothpick inserted in the center comes out clean. Uncover and let cool in the pot. When cool enough to handle, loosen the sides and lift out carefully with a flexible spatula, or loosen sides and invert the pot slightly and remove with your hand (you could hold a small piece of foil or waxed paper).

Fried Apples

Use these apples as a topping, a filling, or alone topped with whipped cream.
3 pounds granny smith apples, peeled, cored, and sliced
1 teaspoon cinnamon
Dash of fresh grated nutmeg, optional
3 tablespoons cornstarch

1 cup granulated sugar
1 to 2 tablespoons of butter, cut in small pieces

Place apple slices in the crock pot; stir in remaining ingredients and dot with the butter. Cover and cook on low for about 6 hours, or until apples are tender but not mushy. Stir about halfway through cooking. Makes 2 1/2 to 3 cups.

Garlic Chicken With Cabbage

1 whole chicken
1/2-to 1whole red or white onion chopped
3-8 garlic cloves or use garlic salt/powder to you liking
Salt and pepper to taste

Season chicken and place in crock pot. Add onion and garlic cloves and salt and pepper. Fill crock pot 1/4-way with water, cover and cook on high 6-8 hours. The chicken should fall off of the bone. During the last hour of cooking the chicken, cut up 1 head of green cabbage, core removed. Place in a large pot of pan with a shallow amount of water...1/2-to 1-cup. Add two tablespoons of butter or margarine and sprinkle liberally with garlic salt and pepper. Cover and cook on med-high heat for 20-30 minutes. Once chicken and cabbage are done, place some cabbage in a bowl and top with chicken and some of the chicken broth. You can alter any of the seasonings and the butter or margarine to your satisfaction.

Garlic Pepper Chicken Parmesan

4 chicken leg quarters
2 tbsp. Mrs. Dash's gallant garlic's roasted garlic pepper seasoning
1 cans Del Monte zucchini with tomato sauce
3 oz. shredded mozzarella cheese

Put chicken in pot. Sprinkle with seasoning. Pour zucchini with tomato sauce over chicken. Cook for 6 hours on high. Sprinkle with cheese and cook until cheese melts - about 30 mins.

Garlic Roasted Chicken

5 pound roasting chicken
Salt
Pepper
Paprika
5 garlic cloves, minced
1/4 pound sweet butter
1/2 cup chicken broth

Sprinkle the chicken, inside and out, with salt, pepper and paprika. Spread half of the garlic in the cavity and spread the rest on the outside of the bird. Place the bird in the crock pot and place a few pats of butter on its breast. Add the remaining ingredients and cook on low for 6 to 8 hours. Serve the garlic butter sauce with the chicken.

German Potato Salad

2 potatoes, sliced
1/2 c. onions, chopped
1/2 c. celery sliced
1/4 c. green peppers, diced
1/4 c. vinegar
1/4 c. oil
Chopped parsley
Sliced bacon, cooked and crumbled

Combine all ingredients except parsley and bacon. Add salt and pepper to taste. Stir and cook for 5-6 hours in crock pot. Add sugar if needed. Garnish with bacon and parsley.

Ginger Brown Bread

1 (14-oz.) pkg. gingerbread mix
1/4 cup yellow corn meal
1 tsp. salt
1-1/2 cups milk
1/2 cup raisins

Combine gingerbread mix with corn meal and salt in large bowl; stir in milk until mixture is evenly moist. Beat at medium speed with electric mixer for 2 min. stir in raisins. Pour into a greased and floured 7 or 7 cup mold. Cover with foil and tie. Put a trivet or metal rack in crock pot. Pour 2 cups hot water in the pot. Place the filled mold on the rack or the trivet. Cover the pot and cook on high for 3 - 4 hours or until the bread is done. Remove from pot and cool on a rack for 5 min. loosen the edges with a knife and turn out on a rack and cool slightly. Serve warm with butter or cream cheese.

Glazed Cocktail Sausages

3/4 cup apricot preserves
1/4 cup prepared yellow mustard
2 scallions chopped
1/2 pound precooked mini smoked sausages (the ones with cheese in them will work also)

In a 1-quart mini electric crock pot; mix together the preserves and mustard. Stir in scallions and sausages. Cover, plug in the cooker and cook for 3 hours or until very hot. Remove the cover, stir to mix and serve immediately with toothpicks; keep the heat on for another 30-60 minutes if desired while serving.

Grape Jelly Meatballs

1 1/2 cups chili sauce
1 cup grape jelly
1 to 3 teaspoons Dijon mustard
1 pound lean ground beef
1 egg, lightly beaten
3 tablespoons fine dry bread crumbs
1/2 teaspoon salt

Combine chili sauce, jelly, and mustard in crock pot and stir well. Cook, covered, on high while preparing meatballs. Combine remaining ingredients and mix thoroughly. Shape into 30 meatballs. Bake meatballs in a preheated 400 degree oven for 15 to 20 minutes; drain well. Add meatballs to sauce, stir to coat, cover and cook on low for 6 to 10 hours.

Greek Chicken

6 skinless chicken breasts
1 lg. cans tomato sauce
1 sm. cans tomato puree
1 cans sliced mushrooms
1 cans ripe olives
1 tbsp. garlic
1 tbsp. lemon juice
1 tsp. oregano
1 onion, chopped
1/2 c. wine or brandy (optional)
2 c. rice

Salt to taste wash and remove fat from chicken. Bake in 350 degree oven for about an hour. Meanwhile, combine all other ingredients except rice. Put chicken and sauce in a crock pot on low heat and cook for at least 4 hours to blend flavors. Before serving, cook rice according to on box. Serve chicken and sauce over rice. Serves 6.

Greek Stew

3 pounds of stewing beef
1 1/2 pounds small onions (about 7)
3 cloves garlic, minced
28 oz. can tomatoes
1/2 cup beef stock
5 1/2 oz. can tomato paste
2 tbs red wine vinegar
2 tsp dried oregano
1/2 tsp each salt & pepper
1/2 cup all purpose flour
1/2 cup cold water
1 sweet green pepper, chopped
1/2 cup crumbled feta cheese
2 tbsp. chopped fresh parsley

Cut beef into 1 inch cubes, trimming off any fat cut onions into wedges leaving root end intact. Put meat & onions into crock pot along with garlic & tomatoes. Combine beef stock, vinegar, oregano, salt & pepper and add to crock pot, stirring gently to blend. Cook on low for 8-9 hours or high for 6 hours. Add flour & water mixture and chopped green pepper. Cook on high for 15 minutes or until thickened. Serve sprinkled with feta & parsley.

Green Bean And Potato Casserole

About 6 cups fresh trimmed and cut green beans (about 2 pounds) or 2 16-ounce packages frozen cut green beans
4 to 6 medium red-skinned potatoes, sliced about 1/4-inch
1 large onion, sliced
1 teaspoon dried dill weed
1 teaspoon salt
1/2 teaspoon pepper
1 can cream of chicken soup or other cream soup, undiluted, or use about 1 cup of homemade seasoned white sauce, velouté or cheese sauce margarine
Spray the Crockpot with cooking spray or lightly grease with butter or margarine. Layer sliced potatoes, sliced onion and green beans, sprinkling with dill and salt and pepper as you go. Dot with margarine, about 1 tablespoon total, and add about 2 tablespoons of water. Cover and cook on high for 4 hours (low, about 8 hours). Stir in soup or sauce; turn to low and cook an additional 30 minutes or leave on warm (smart-pot) until serving time or up to 4 hours. Serves 6 to 8. Note: add bits of cooked bacon for extra flavor.

Green Chile-Stuffed Chicken Breasts

With the cheese mixture in the center, these chicken breasts come out tender and moist.
4 boneless, skinned chicken breast halves, pounded thin
3 ounces cream cheese
3/4 cups shredded cheddar or Monterey jack cheese
4 ounces green chilies
1/2 teaspoon chili powder
Salt and pepper to taste
1 can cream of mushroom soup
1/2 cup hot enchilada sauce

Combine cream cheese, shredded cheese, chilies, chili powder and salt and pepper. Place a generous dollop on each flattened chicken breast, and then roll up. Place chicken rolls in the crock pot, seam-side down. Top chicken breast rolls with remaining cheese mixture, soup, and enchilada sauce. Cover and cook on low for 6 to 7 hours. Serves 4.

Ham Broccoli Chowder

2 tbsp. flour
1 sm. can evaporated milk
2 c. ham, diced
1 pkg. frozen chopped broccoli
1/4 c. onion, minced
1 c. Swiss cheese, grated
2 c. water
1 c. light cream

Mix flour and evaporated milk in cooker. Add other ingredients except cream. Cook on low 7 hours or on automatic for 4 hours. Before serving, stir in cream and heat. Yields: 6 servings.

Hamburger Dip

2 pounds lean ground beef
1 cup chopped onion
2 cloves garlic, minced or 1/4 teaspoon garlic powder
Salt to taste
2 cans (8-ounces each) tomato sauce
1/2 cup ketchup
1 1/2 teaspoons oregano
2 teaspoons white granulated sugar
2 package (8-ounces each) cream cheese, softened and cut in cubes

2/3 cup grated parmesan cheese
1 teaspoon mild chili powder

In skillet, brown ground beef with onion, discard fat. Pour browned meat and onion into crock pot. Add garlic, salt, tomato sauce, ketchup, oregano, sugar, cream cheese, parmesan cheese and chili powder. Set crock pot on low until cream cheese has melted and is thoroughly blended, 1 1/2 to 2 hours. Stir, taste and adjust seasoning if desired. Serve with cube French bread or tortilla chips. If spicier dip is desired, use hot chili powder in place of mild chili powder. Finely chopped jalapenos may be added, if desired.

Healthy Crockpot Chicken Creole

3 lbs. chicken thighs or breasts, skinned
1 cup celery, diced
1 red bell pepper, sliced
1 green bell pepper, sliced
1 onion, sliced
1 cans sliced mushrooms
1 cans tomatoes
1 tsp. garlic powder
3 pkg. sugar substitute
1 tsp. Cajun seasoning
1/2 tsp. paprika
Salt & pepper to taste
Louisiana hot sauce to taste
2 cups minute rice, cooked

Place chicken in bottom of crock pot. Combine remaining ingredients (except rice) & add to crock pot. Cook on high 4 to 5 hours or on low 7-8 hours. Cook rice according to package direction. Spoon Creole mixture over hot cooked rice.

Hearty Beef Dip

8 ounces cream cheese, cubed
1 1/4 ounces sliced dried beef, diced
2 tablespoons green onion, chopped
1/4 cup milk
1/4 cup pecans, chopped
1 garlic clove

Combine cream cheese and milk in greased crock pot. Cover and heat until cheese is melted, 30 to 60 minutes. Add remaining ingredients; stir thoroughly. Cover and heat 30 minutes.

Serve with crackers or bread pieces.

Hearty Chili

1 pound ground turkey
1/2 ground chuck
30 oz. tomato sauce
24 oz. v-8 (tomato-vegetable juice)
1/2 c. chopped onion
1/2 c. chopped celery
1 tbsp. chili powder
1 c. chopped green pepper
1 c. chopped mushrooms
1 sm. jalapeno pepper (optional)
14 oz. stewed tomatoes
1/2 c. uncooked wild rice
2/3 c. brown sugar
14 oz. chili beans
1 oz. chili seasoning mix

Brown ground turkey and ground beef. Drain well. Place all other ingredients in a crock pot and add the meat. Cook on low for 6 to 9 hours. Serve with crackers or cornbread.

Home-Style Bread Pudding

2 eggs, slightly beaten
2 1/4 cups milk
1 teaspoon vanilla
1/2 teaspoon cinnamon
1/4 teaspoon salt
2 cups 1-inch bread cubes
1/2 cup brown sugar
1/2 cup raisins or chopped dates

in medium mixing bowl, combine eggs with milk, vanilla, cinnamon, salt, bread, sugar, and raisins or dates. Pour into 1 1/2-quart baking or soufflé dish. Place metal trivet (or aluminum foil shaped in a ring to keep the dish off the bottom of the pot) or rack in bottom of crock pot. Add 1/2 cup hot water. Set baking dish on trivet. Cover pot; cook on high for about 2 hours. Serve pudding warm or cool. Makes 4 to 6 servings.

Honeyed Chicken Wings

3 lb. chicken wings
Salt & pepper, to taste
1 c. honey
1/2 c. soy sauce
2 tbsp. vegetable oil
2 tbsp. ketchup
1/2 garlic clove, minced

Cut off and discard chicken wing tips. Cut each wing into 2 parts and sprinkle with salt and pepper. Combine remaining ingredients and mix well. Place wings in crock pot and pour sauce over. Cook 6 to 8 hours on low.

Hot Artichoke Dip

6 ounces artichoke hearts, marinated
1/3 cup mayonnaise
1 tablespoon pimento, diced (optional)
1/2 cup parmesan cheese, grated
1/3 cup sour cream
1/8 teaspoon garlic powder

Drain and chop artichoke hearts. Combine all ingredients and place in crock pot. Cover and heat 30 to 60 minutes until hot. Serve with tortilla chips or assorted crackers.

Hot Broccoli Dip

1 (10 oz.) chopped frozen broccoli, thawed
1 stick margarine
1 med. onion, chopped
1 (10 3/4 oz.) cans of cream of mushroom soup
14 oz. Velveeta cheese, cut up
1 to 2 1/2 oz. can mushroom stems and pieces

Combine first 3 ingredients in a sauté pan and cook until onions are clear. Transfer to the crock pot. Add soup, cheese, and mushrooms, heat on low for about 1 1/2 to 2 hours, or until cheese is melted and mixture is hot. Dip with large corn chips or can be poured over baked potatoes.

Hot Caramel Apples

4 lg. tart apples, cored
1/2 c. apple juice
8 tbsp brown sugar
12 red-hot candies
4 tbsp butter or margarine
8 caramels
1/4 tsp. ground cinnamon

Peel about 3/4 inch off the top of each apple; place in crock. Pour juice over apples. Fill the center of each apple with 2 tbsp of sugar, 3 red-hots, 1tblspoon of butter and 2 caramels. Sprinkle with cinnamon. Cover and cook on low for 4-6 hours or until apples are tender. May serve immediately with whipped cream if desired. Makes 4 servings.

Hot Chicken Sandwiches

12 eggs
1 loaf of bread (cubed)
2 large (or 3 small) boiler chickens (reserve some broth for use in recipe)
Salt to taste pepper to taste

Boil the chickens until done and let cool. When the chicken meat is completely cool to the touch, pick the chicken meat from the bones and set aside. Reserve a little of the broth for later. Cube the loaf of bread and put it in a large bowl. Mix in the 12 eggs with the cubed bread. Add the chicken meat you picked from the bone and enough broth from the chicken to moisten. Add salt and pepper to your own taste. Mix well. Spread mixture into a lightly greased casserole dish and bake in a preheated 350 degrees f (175 degrees c) oven for 30 minutes. Or spray a crock pot with cooking spray to prevent sticking and pour in the chicken mixture. Let cook on low for about 6 hours. Serve by scooping onto buns. Makes 12 to 18 servings

Hot Chili Con Queso

1 1/2 cups half-and-half, scalded
1/2 pound grated Monterrey jack cheese
1/2 pound grated sharp process cheese
1 tablespoon butter
1/2 onion, minced
1 medium clove garlic, minced
1/4 cup dry white wine or low-sodium stock
1/4 cup flour
1/4 cup water

1 can chopped green chile peppers (4 oz)
1 to 2 tablespoons chopped jalapeno (more or less depending on taste)
Salt and pepper
Dash cayenne pepper

Pour scalded half-and-half into buttered crock pot. Turn to high and stir in cheeses.
In small skillet, sauté onion and garlic in butter until onion is tender. Add wine or stock and stir well. Add to cheese mixture. Combine flour with water and stir in. cook covered on high for 30 minutes, or until cheese begins to melt. Turn to low and cook about 4 to 6 hours, stirring 2 or 3 times during the first hour and occasionally after that. If the mixture is too thin, mix 2 tablespoons of flour with 2 tablespoons of water and add. Serve warm with tortilla chips and/or other dippers.

Hot Dog And Bacon Rollups

2 pkg. hot dogs cut in half
Brown sugar
1 lb. bacon, cut into in the middle

Take a piece of hot dog and piece of bacon, wrap bacon around hot dog. Stick a toothpick through bacon to hold. Place one layer in bottom of crock pot and cover with brown sugar. Repeat until all the hot dogs have been used. Cook 3 to 4 hours.

Hot Dog Hors D'oeuvres

2 (1 lb.) pkgs all beef hot dogs, sliced in half
1 lb. bacon, sliced in half
Brown sugar

Wrap each hot dog half with bacon strip. Fasten with toothpick. Layer in crock pot, sprinkling each layer with a thin layer of brown sugar. Repeat layers until hot dogs run out. Cook on low for 2-3 hours, stirring gently with wooden spoon every 30 minutes.

Hot Fruit Compote

1 can peaches, drained
1 can pears, drained
1 cans pineapple chunks, drained
1 cup brown sugar
1 tsp. cinnamon
1/2 stick margarine (4oz)
1 cans cherry pie filling

Cut all fruit into bite-size pieces. Add rest of ingredients. Stir all together. Cover and cook on low 3 to 6 hours. Use as a side dish for breakfast or a meal, or as a topping for a dessert.

Hot 'N' Spicy Pecans

1/4 cup butter cut in pieces (4 oz)
6 cups pecans
2 teaspoons chili powder
1/2 teaspoon onion salt
1/2 teaspoon garlic powder

Place cut up butter in crock pot and heat, uncovered, on high until melted (15 to 20 minutes). Add pecans; stir to coat. Cover and cook on high 30 minutes. Uncover and cook on high 2 1/2 hours longer, stirring occasionally. Sprinkle with the seasonings and toss to coat; spread on a baking sheet to cool. Store in an airtight container in the refrigerator for up to 6 weeks, or freeze for up to 3 months. Serve at room temperature or warm.

Hot Spinach Dip

2 (10 oz.) pkgs. frozen chopped spinach
1 lg. jar jalapeno cheez whiz
1 can cream of mushroom soup
1 (3 oz.) pkg. cream cheese
2 tbsp. dried minced onion

Thaw spinach completely. Drain, and squeeze as much moisture as possible from spinach. Combine all ingredients in the crock pot and cook on low about 2 hours, until hot (stir a few times to blend well). Keep warm in crock pot or chafing dish. Serve with corn chips or crackers.

Indian Pudding

3 c. milk
1/2 c. cornmeal
1/2 tsp. salt
3 eggs
1/4 c. light brown sugar
1/3 c. molasses
2 tbsp. butter
1/2 tsp. cinnamon
1/4 tsp. allspice
1/2 tsp. ginger

Lightly grease Crockpot. Preheat on high for 20 minutes. Meanwhile bring milk, cornmeal and salt to a boil. Boil, stirring constantly, for 5 minutes. Cover and simmer an additional 10 minutes. In a large bowl, combine remaining ingredients. Gradually beat in hot cornmeal mixture and whisk until smooth. Pour into crock and cook on high for 2 to 3 hours or low for 6 to 8 hours.

Italian Green Beans

1/3-1/2 lb. sweet Italian sausage
15 oz can stewed tomatoes, chopped
4 cans (8 oz) sliced mushrooms (do not drain)
1/4-1/2 tsp. onion &/or garlic powders
1/2 tsp. basil &/or oregano
3 (1 lb.) cans Italian style green beans, 2 of them drained
1/2 cup parmesan cheese

Brown sausage and drain. Add all ingredients except green beans. Mix thoroughly and simmer for 15 minutes. Add green beans and mix. Bake at 250 degrees in a covered casserole for 30 minutes to 2 hours; or in a crock pot on low up to 3 hours.

Jerk Chicken

1 large onion, cut into 8 pieces
1 generous tablespoon chopped crystallized ginger
1/2 to 1 habanera pepper, seeded, deveined, and finely minced
1/2 teaspoon ground allspice
2 tablespoons dry mustard
1 teaspoon freshly ground black pepper
2 tablespoons red wine or balsamic vinegar
2 tablespoons soy sauce
2 cloves garlic, crushed and minced
3 to 4 pounds chicken tenders

Combine onion and ginger in a food processor; process until finely chopped. Add remaining ingredients, except chicken, and pulse until well combined. Place chicken in a 3 1/2-quart (or larger) crock pot and cover with sauce. Cover, set on low, and cook for 6 to 8 hours or until chicken is tender (3 to 4 hours on high). 4 servings.

Lamb

2 tablespoons olive oil
2 (7 bone) racks of lamb, trimmed, fat reserved
Salt and pepper to taste

4 cloves garlic, minced
1 large onion, diced
4 carrots, diced
1 cup celery tops
1 cup port wine
1 cup red wine
1 (14.5 ounce) can low-sodium chicken broth
5 sprigs fresh spearmint
3 sprigs fresh rosemary
1 cup mint apple jelly
2 tablespoons olive oil
Salt and pepper to taste
1 tablespoon garlic, minced
1/4 cup pink bread crumbs
2 tablespoons olive oil
4 sprigs fresh mint

To make demi-glace:
Heat 2 tablespoons olive oil in a medium skillet over medium heat, and add trimmings from lamb. Season with salt and pepper. brown the fat, reduce heat, and add 4 cloves minced garlic, onion, carrots, celery leaves, port, red wine, and chicken broth. Transfer the mixture to a crock pot, and simmer on low 8 hours, or overnight. Strain the crock pot mixture into a saucepan over medium-low heat. Mix in the spearmint, rosemary, and mint jelly, and simmer, adding more port, wine, or broth as needed, until mixture leaves a syrup-like coating on the back of a spoon. Strain once more, and keep warm while lamb roasts.

To roast lamb:
Place a cast iron or oven-proof skillet in the oven, and preheat to 450 degrees. Rub lamb with 2 tablespoons olive oil, salt, pepper, and garlic. Coat with panko bread crumbs. Carefully remove the heated skillet from the oven, warm 2 tablespoons olive oil in the skillet, and sear lamb on both sides. Return the skillet with the lamb to the preheated oven, and continue cooking 5 to 10 minutes, to an internal temperature of 145 degrees. Pour a small amount of the demi-glace on platter and arrange lamb crises-crossed. Drizzle with more demi-glace, and garnish with fresh mint to serve.

Lamb Stew

1 pound boneless lamb shoulder, cut into 2 inch pieces
2 cups diced carrots
5 large potatoes, peeled and diced
1/2 sweet yellow onion, chopped
3 cloves garlic, minced
2 cups beef stock
1 pinch seasoned or to taste
Ground black pepper to taste
1 pinch paprika, or to taste
1 pinch dried thyme, or to taste

1 (1.5 fluid ounce) jigger Irish whiskey
1 cup frozen peas

Place lamb shoulder, carrots, potatoes, onion, garlic, beef stock, seasoned salt, pepper, paprika, thyme, and Irish whiskey in a crock pot. Cook on low for 6 to 7 hours. Add peas about 15 minutes before serving.

Lasagna

1 box rigatoni, cooked
1 1/2 lbs. ground chuck, browned & drained
1 lg. pkg. sliced pepperoni
1 green pepper, chopped
2 lg. pkgs. mozzarella cheese
2 lg. cans pizza sauce
1 med. onion, chopped
2 lg. cans mushrooms
Green olives, sliced

Begin with layer of sauce on bottom of crock pot. Stir all remaining ingredients together. Place in crock pot and cook on low for 5 hours.

Lazy Crockpot Chicken

1 pkg. boneless chicken breasts
1 can cream of mushroom soup
1/4 c. flour
1 jar sliced mushrooms
Salt, pepper and paprika

Rinse chicken breasts. Put salt, pepper and paprika on both sides. Place in crock pot. Mix other ingredients together. Add to crock pot. Cook on low all day. Serve over noodles, rice, or mashed potatoes.

Lemon Baked Chicken

16 ounces skinned and boned uncooked chicken breasts, cut into 4 pieces
1 lemon
1 teaspoon lemon pepper
1 teaspoon paprika

Place chicken pieces in a crock pot. Squeeze juice of half a lemon over chicken. Sprinkle lemon pepper and paprika over top. Cut remaining lemon half into thin slices. Arrange slices around chicken. Cover and cook on high for 4 hours.

Lemon Garlic Chicken

3 pounds chicken
1/2 cup lemon juice
1/2 cup garlic cloves, crushed
1 teaspoon seasoned salt
1 teaspoon poultry seasoning
2 dashes Tabasco
1 cup white wine

Skin and cut up chicken. Combine with other ingredients in crock pot. Set on low. Upon return from work, debone chicken. Serve over rice. If you freeze chicken pieces separately, and mix up other ingredients the night before, you can dump it all together quickly in the morning. And if you start with frozen chicken it doesn't fall apart.

Lemon Pepper Chicken

5 boneless skinless chicken breasts (or any chicken pieces)
Lemon pepper seasoning
2 tbsp. melted or squeeze margarine

Put chicken in crock pot. Sprinkle generously with seasoning. Pour margarine over chicken. Cook on low for 10 hrs. Or on high for 6 hrs.

Lemon Poppy Seed Upside Down Cake

1 pkg. lemon-poppy seed bread mix
1 egg 8 ounces light sour cream
1/2 cup water

Sauce:
1 tablespoon butter
3/4 cup water
1/2 cup sugar
Juice from one lemon (about 1/4 cup)

Mix the first 4 ingredients together until well moistened. Spread batter in a lightly greased 3 1/2 quart crock pot. Combine sauce ingredients in a small saucepan; bring to a boil. Pour boiling mixture over the batter; cover and cook on high for 2 to 2 1/2 hours. Edges will be slightly browned. Turn heat off and leave in the pot for about 30 minutes with cover slightly ajar. When cool enough to handle, hold a large plate over the top of the pot then invert.

Lemon Rosemary Chicken

1/2 c. lemon juice
1 tbsp. vegetable oil
1 garlic clove, crushed
1 teaspoon. Dried rosemary
1/4 teaspoon. Salt
1/4 teaspoon. Pepper
1 1/2 to 2 lbs. boneless, skinless chicken breasts
In a large food storage bag, place lemon juice, oil, garlic, rosemary, salt and pepper. Add chicken. Close bag and marinate in refrigerator 4 hours or overnight, turning bag frequently. Place chicken in the crock pot and pour marinade over. Cover and cook for 6 to 8 hours, or until tender, basting occasionally with the marinade, if possible. You may add frozen broccoli and carrots about 1 to 1 1/2 hours before done. Serves 4 to 6.

Lemon Tarragon Chicken With Asparagus

1 pound frozen chicken breasts, boneless
1/4 cup lemon juice
1/4 cup chicken stock
1 teaspoon tarragon (dried)
1 package frozen asparagus (or fresh partially cooked)
2 tablespoons flour
1/2 cup heavy or whipping cream
Salt and pepper to taste

Put frozen chicken breasts in crock pot and add lemon juice, broth, and tarragon. Cook on low 6 hours. Add asparagus; whisk cream and flour together and add. Cook another hour on high or until asparagus is tender and sauce is thickened. Serve over noodles or rice. Artichokes are good in this too!

Lo-Cal Crock Pot Chicken

2 med. onions, thinly sliced
2-3 lb. chicken, cut up and skinned
2 cloves garlic, minced
1 lg. cans tomatoes
1 tsp. salt
1/4 tsp. pepper
1/2 tsp. oregano, crushed
1/2 tsp. basil
1/2 tsp. celery seed
1 bay leaf

Layer in order and cook on low 6-8 hours, or on high 2 1/2 - 4 hours.

Low Fat Chicken & Veggie Bake

8 boneless, skinless chicken breasts
2 cans whole potatoes, drained
1 tsp garlic powder
1 bottle fat free Italian salad dressing
1 pkg frozen veggies
1 can water chestnuts (optional)
Salt & pepper

Sprinkle chicken breasts with salt, pepper and garlic. Put chicken in bottom of crock pot. Add remaining ingredients. Cook on high for 4-6 hours or on low for 8-10 hours. Serves 8

Low Fat Glazed Chicken In Crock Pot

6 ounces orange juice, frozen concentrate-thawed
3 chicken breasts split
1/2 tsp marjoram
1 dash ground nutmeg
1 dash garlic powder (optional)
1/4 cup water
2 tbsp cornstarch

Combine thawed orange juice concentrate (not regular orange juice) in bowl along with the marjoram, garlic powder and nutmeg. Split the chicken breasts to make 6 serving sizes. Dip pieces into the orange juice to coat completely. Place in crock pot. Pour the remaining orange juice mixture over the chicken. Cover and cook on low for 7-9 hours, or cook on high for 4 hours if you wish. Precise cooking time is not important in crock pot cooking. When chicken is done, remove to serving platter. Pour the sauce that remains into a saucepan. Mix the cornstarch and water and stir into the juice in pan. Cook over medium heat, stirring constantly, until thick and bubbly. Serve the sauce over the chicken.

Luscious Lemon Cheesecake

Crust:
1 cup vanilla wafer crumbs
1/2 teaspoon lemon zest
1 tablespoons sugar
3 tablespoons butter, melted

Filling:
16 ounces cream cheese
2/3 cup sugar
2 large eggs
1 tablespoon flour or cornstarch
1 teaspoon fresh lemon zest
2 tablespoons fresh lemon juice

Combine crust ingredients. Pat into a 7-inch spring form pan. Beat cream cheese and sugar together until smooth; beat in eggs and continue beating on medium speed of a hand-held electric mixer for about 3 minutes. Beat in remaining ingredients and continue beating for about 1 minute. Pour batter into the prepared crust. Place the cheesecake on a rack in the crock pot. Cover and cook on high for 2 1/2 to 3 hours. Let stand in the covered pot after turning it off for about an hour or 2, until cool enough to handle. Cool thoroughly before removing pan sides. Chill in the refrigerator before serving, and refrigerate any leftovers.

Macaroni Pie

8 oz. box (cooked) macaroni
3 c. grated cheese
1 (16 oz.) can of evaporated milk
1 1/2 c. sweet milk
2 eggs
1/4 c. margarine
1 tsp. sugar
Salt and pepper to taste

Combine cooked macaroni with other ingredients and pour into a greased Crockpot. Cook 3 1/2 hours on medium heat.

Manhattan Meatballs

1 lb ground beef
1 lb. mild pork sausage (or use all beef)
2 c. soft bread crumbs or 1 1/2 c. oatmeal
2 eggs
1/2 c. chopped onion
2 tbsp. parsley
2 tsp. salt
1/2 tsp. garlic salt sauce:
1 (12 oz) jar apricot preserves
1/2 c. barbecue sauce

Mix first 8 ingredients together and form meatballs. Brown in skillet, or in oven at 450 degrees for 15 minutes. Heat sauce, pour over meatballs. Bake at 350 degrees for 25 minutes or cook in crock pot. Can be served over rice or as an appetizer with toothpicks. Makes 4 or 5 dozen.

Maple Flavored Barbecue Chicken

1 c. ketchup
1/2 c. maple flavored syrup
2 tbsp. prepared mustard
2 tbsp. Worcestershire sauce
2 tsp. lemon juice
1/2 tsp. chili powder
1/4 tsp. garlic powder
4 boneless, skinned chicken breasts

Place all ingredients in crock pot and cook on low for about 7 to 8 hours or until chicken is done. Remove meat, shred and return to sauce. Place on buns for sandwiches or serve over hot rice. Serves 4 to 6.

Maple Glazed Sweet Potatoes

5 medium sweet potatoes
1/4 cup brown sugar
1/4 cup pure maple syrup
1/4 cup apple cider
Dash salt and pepper to taste

Peel sweet potatoes and cut into 1/4 to 1/2-inch thick slices; place in crock pot. Whisk remaining ingredients together and pour over potatoes. Cover and cook on low 7 to 9 hours. Stir a few times, if possible, to keep them coated. Serves 4.

Mariner Fondue

2 cans (10 3/4 oz each) condensed cream of celery soup
2 c. grated sharp process cheese
1 c. chunked cooked lobster
1/2 c. chopped cooked shrimp
1/2 c. chopped cooked crabmeat
1/4 c. finely chopped, cooked scallops
Dash paprika
Dash cayenne pepper

1 loaf of French bread, cut into 1 inch cubes

Combine all ingredients except bread cubes in lightly greased crock-pot; stir thoroughly. Cover and cook on high for 1 hour or until cheese is melted. Turn to low for serving. Using fondue forks, dip bread cubes into fondue. Makes about 1 1/2 qts.

Marmalade Glazed Carrots

1 package (32oz) fresh baby carrots
1/2 cup marmalade
1 tablespoon water
2 tablespoon brown sugar
1 tablespoon butter
1/2 teaspoon cinnamon
1/4 teaspoon nutmeg
1 tablespoons cornstarch
2 tablespoons water
Salt and pepper to taste

Combine all ingredients in crock pot and cook on low for 7 to 9 hours, until carrots are tender.
About 15 minutes before serving, make a paste of the cornstarch and cold water; stir into carrots
Taste and adjust seasonings. Serves 4 to 6 as a side dish.

Meatballs

2 pounds ground beef
1 medium onion-grated or minced
20 Ritz crackers, crushed
1/4 teaspoon black pepper
1/4 teaspoon garlic salt
1/2 teaspoon dry mustard
2 large eggs, beaten
1 1/2 cups bottled barbecue sauce
3/4 cup tomato paste
1 teaspoon liquid smoke
1/3 cup catsup
1/3 cup brown sugar
1/2 cup water or as needed

In a large bowl combine the ground beef, onion, crushed crackers, pepper, garlic salt, dry mustard and eggs. Squish the mixture together by hand until well mixed and form into walnut sized balls. Place them on a flat wire rack in a roasting pan or a large cake pan. Bake the meatballs in a 350 degree oven for 15 minutes, turn and bake for 15 minutes more. In a crock pot combine the remaining ingredients. Cook on high 30 minutes. Add the meatballs and simmer for several hours. Makes about 60 meatballs.

Meatballs Over Buttered Noodles

2 (10.75 ounce) cans condensed cream of celery soup
2 (10.5 ounce) cans condensed French onion soup
1 (16 ounce) container sour cream
6 pounds frozen Italian-style meatballs
2 (16 ounce) packages uncooked egg noodles
1/2 cup butter

In a large crock pot, mix together the cream of celery soup, French onion soup, and sour cream. Stir in the meatballs. Cook on high heat for 3-4 hours. Bring a large pot of lightly salted water to a boil. Add pasta and cook for 8 to 10 minutes or until al dente; drain. In a large bowl, toss the pasta with butter. Serve meatballs and sauce over the cooked pasta.

Meatloaf

3 lbs. ground turkey or chicken
1 lb. ground hamburger
1 c. instant rice
1/4 c. a-1
2 whole eggs
1/4 c. flour, bread crumbs or crushed crackers or chips
Salt, pepper, onion powder, garlic powder to taste

Combine all ingredients. Form into ball. Wrap well in foil. Poke small holes in bottom side of ball. Place in crock pot on canning lids or something that will keep the meat above any drippings. Cook on low 8 hours.

Mediterranean Style Chicken

6 skinless and boneless chicken breasts 1 large can tomato sauce
1 small can tomato puree
1 cans sliced mushrooms
1 cans ripe olives, sliced or whole
1 tablespoon garlic
1 tablespoon lemon juice
1 teaspoon oregano
1 onion, chopped

1/2 cup wine or brandy (optional)
Cooked rice
Salt to taste

Wash and remove excess fat from chicken. Combine all ingredients in the crock pot, except the rice. Cover and cook on low for 6 to 8 hours. Serve chicken and sauce over rice. Serves 6.

Mexican Cheese Dip

1/2 pound Velveeta
1 teaspoon taco seasoning (optional)
1/2 cans rotel tomatoes with chilies

Cube cheese and place in crock pot. Cover and heat 30 to 60 minutes, until melted, stirring occasionally. Stir in tomatoes and seasoning. Cover and continue heating 30 minutes. Serve with tortilla chips or corn chips.

Mexican Chicken In Crockpot

Chicken pieces
Taco seasoning

Let cook all day on low or several hours on high. Serve as chicken tacos or with aside dish as the main course. Super simple.

Mexican Chili

2 (15 1/2 oz.) cans red kidney beans, drained
1 (28 oz.) can tomatoes, cut up
1 c. chopped celery
1 c. chopped onion
1 (6 oz.) can tomato paste
1/2 c. chopped green pepper
1 (4 oz.) can green chili peppers, drained and chopped
2 tbsp. sugar
1 bay leaf
1/2 tsp. garlic powder
1 tsp. salt
1 tsp. dried, crushed marjoram
Dash of pepper
1 lb. ground beef

In skillet brown ground beef and drain. In crockery cooker combine all ingredients. Cover, cook on low heat for 8 to 10 hours. Remove bay leaf and stir before serving. Approximately 10 servings and great with corn bread!

Mint Butter Wafers

2 t. butter
1/4 c. milk
1 pkg. white frosting mix (dry)
3 drops peppermint flavoring

Melt butter and milk together in a covered cooker on high. Stir in frosting and cook 1 to 2 minutes more. Add flavoring. Turn to low and drop by teaspoonfuls onto waxed paper. Makes 5 dozen.

Mixed Vegetable Bake

2 cans creamed corn, 17 oz each
2 cans green beans; cut, 16 oz each
2 cans peas, 16 oz each
1 cans tomatoes, 17 oz
1/2 cup mayonnaise
1 teaspoon tarragon
1 teaspoon basil
1/2 teaspoon salt
Pepper

Combine all ingredients in removable liner, mix well to blend herbs. Place liner incase. Cover and cook on low 4-6 hours.

No Bean Chili

2 pounds ground beef, or cubed lean stew beef
1 (8 oz) can tomato sauce
1 (6 oz) can tomato paste
1 (16 oz) can stewed tomatoes, optional
2 tablespoons chili powder
1 1/2 teaspoons salt
1 teaspoon hot pepper sauce or more

Combine all ingredients in crock pot. Cover and cook on low for 8-10 hours. (Add a can of your favorite beans if you wish.) Serves 4 to 6.

Old Fashioned Crockpot Apple Butter

14 cooking apples (Winesap)
2 1/2 c. sugar
1 c. apple juice
1 tbsp. cinnamon
1 tbsp. cloves
1 tsp. allspice

Wash and core apples; cut in 1/4 pieces. Slightly grease Crockpot, put in apples and apple juice. Cook on high for 5 hours. Add other ingredients and cook for 6 hours on high. Stir each hour. Pack in 1/2 pint jars and seal. Makes 5 (1/2 pint) jars.

One Pot Chicken And Gravy

Boneless, skinless chicken breasts
Potatoes, quartered, with jackets
About 6 stalks celery
1/2 pkg baby carrots
1 can cream of chicken soup*
1 pkg dry onion soup mix

Place vegetables on bottom of crock pot. Brown chicken breasts in Pam or vegetable spray. Place over vegetables. Cover with the cream of chicken soup, undiluted. Sprinkle with dry onion soup mix. Do not add water. Cover and cook all day on low, or 6 hours on high.

Orange Glazed Chicken

6 ounces orange juice, frozen concentrate, thawed
6 chicken breast halves
1/2 teaspoon marjoram
1 dash ground nutmeg
1 dash garlic powder
1/4 cup water
2 tablespoons cornstarch

Combine thawed orange juice concentrate in a bowl with the marjoram, garlic powder and nutmeg. Dip each chicken breast half into the orange juice to coat completely. Place in crock pot. Pour the remaining orange juice mixture over the chicken.
Cover and cook on low for 6-8 hours or on high for about 4 hours.

Orange Burgundy Chicken

2 1/2 to 3 pounds frying chicken, cut up
1/2 cup orange marmalade
1/2 cup orange juice
1/2 cup dry red wine
2 tablespoons cornstarch
2 tablespoons brown sugar, packed
1 tablespoon lemon juice
1 teaspoon salt

Remove skin from chicken. Rinse and place in crock pot. Combine remaining ingredients in a bowl and pour over chicken. Cover and cook on low 6 to 8 hours. Serve with rice and spinach salad. Serves 6.

Orange Glazed Carrots

3 cups thinly sliced carrots
3 tablespoons butter or margarine
2 cups water
3 tablespoons orange marmalade
1/4 teaspoon salt
2 tablespoons chopped pecans

Combine carrots, water, and salt in crock pot. Cover and cook on high 2 to 3 hours or until the carrots are done. Drain well; stir in remaining ingredients. Cover and cook on high 20-30 minutes. Makes 5 to 6 servings.

Oyster Stew

2 qts. Whole milk
1/2 c. butter
2 pts. Fresh oysters
1 1/2 tsp. salt
2 tsp. Worcestershire sauce
In crock pot heat milk on high for 1 1/2 hours. In saucepan, melt butter and add oysters with liquid. Simmer on low until edges of oysters curl. Add seasonings. Combine with the hot milk in crock pot and stew on low for 2-3 hours, stirring occasionally.

Paprikosh

5 large carrots (cubed)
8 large potatoes (cubed)
5 large celery stalks

2 large onions (sliced thin)
3 tablespoons paprika*, salt & pepper to taste

Throw all ingredients into the crock pot, add water to top veggies (it makes a sort of "gravy") and cook on high for 4 hours.

Parmesan Scalloped Potatoes

5 to 6 red potatoes, sliced (about 5 cups sliced)
6 slices turkey bacon or other smoked meat
3 ounces freshly grated parmesan cheese
1 cans condensed cream of mushroom soup
Salt and pepper to taste

Layer all ingredients in lightly buttered 3 1/2-quart crock pot (or use a soufflé dish to fit in a larger crock pot); cover and cook on low for 7 to 9 hours. Adjust seasonings. Serves 4.

Party Hamburger Dip

1 pound hamburger
1 1/2 pounds Velveeta
1 cans rotel tomatoes and chilies
1/2 onion, diced
1 8 - 12 oz fresh mushrooms, sliced

Brown hamburger, mushrooms & onion; drain. Melt Velveeta in crock pot. Add remaining ingredients and simmer (high) for about 30 minutes. Serve with corn chips or crackers. Turn pot to low while serving.

Party Mix

7 cups assorted cereal (oat, rice, wheat in various shapes)
1 cup peanuts, pecans, cashews, or mixed nuts
1 cup mini pretzel sticks
1/2 cup butter or margarine, melted
4 tablespoons Worcestershire sauce
Dash hot pepper sauce
1/2 teaspoon seasoned salt
1/2 teaspoon garlic salt
1/2 teaspoon onion salt

Combine cereals, nuts and pretzels in crock pot. Mix melted butter with remaining ingredients and pour over the cereal mixture, tossing to coat. Cook uncovered on high for 2 hours, stirring about every 30 minutes. Turn to low and cook another 2 to 6 hours. Store in an airtight container. Makes about 10 cups.

Pasta And Broccoli

1 med. onion
1 can cream of mushroom soup
1 lb. Velveeta
1 pkg. frozen broccoli & cauliflower
1 pkg. shell noodles

Mix onion, cream of mushroom soup and Velveeta in a crock pot on high until melted. Add broccoli and cauliflower until hot. Add cooked shells right before serving.

Peach Butter

6 cups unsweetened peaches
3 cups white sugar
1 1/2 cups apricot nectar
2 tablespoons orange or lemon juice
1 teaspoon vanilla

Put peaches through food mill or food processor. Mix all ingredients together well and put in crock pot. Bring to a good boil, uncover and boil until thick or 4 hours, high or low to keep it boiling. When it boils good, remove cover.

Pepper Steak

6 to 8 pepper steaks
1 lg. can mushroom soup
1 tbsp. gravy master
1 lg. onion, sliced in rings
1 med. bell pepper cut in strips
1 c. fresh or canned mushrooms
1 c. flour
4 beef bouillon cubes
Dash of black pepper
4 tbsp. cooking oil

Roll pepper steaks in flour and pepper. Fry in cooking oil over medium heat until lightly browned. Place in crock pot, pour soup over meat. Add the gravy master and bouillon cubes. Arrange vegetables on top. Sprinkle with more pepper, cook on low for 6 to 8 hours or until meat is tender.

Pheasant And Wild Rice

1 cup raw wild raw rice
1 can cream of mushroom soup
1 can cream of chicken soup
1 can mushrooms
2 1/2 cups water
2 pheasants, cut up, flour and brown
1 pkg instant onion soup mix

Mix rice, canned soup, water, mushrooms and water together in crock pot. Place pheasants in crock. Sprinkle with onion soup mix. Cover. Cook on low 6 to 8 hours. Add a splash more water if rice is looking dry towards end of cooking time.

Philippine Chicken

1 chicken, cut up
1 cup water
1/2 cup vinegar
1/4 cup soy sauce
2 cloves garlic, sliced

Put all in crock pot; cook for 6 to 8 hours on low. Serve over rice.

Picante Cheese Dip

1 1/2 pounds ground beef (browned)
1 cans (11 oz.) cream of mushroom soup
2 pound processed cheese (Velveeta)
1 stick margarine
1 onion, chopped
2 tbsp. chili powder
1 cup picante sauce

Brown meat and onion. Drain. Add all ingredients to crock pot and cook on low heat until cheese melts, about 1 1/2 hours. Serve in crock pot with tortilla chips.

Pizza Dip

1 large cream cheese softened
1 jar pizza sauce
1 small can chopped olives
1 medium onion chopped

1 pkg. sliced pepperoni
1 pkg. grated cheese for pizza

Spread cream cheese in bottom of crock pot. Then mix up the pizza sauce, onion, olives and pepperoni and spread on top of the cream cheese. Sprinkle with the pizza cheese and cook on low until the cheese on top melts. Serve with tortilla chips.

Pizza Fondue

1 lb. ground beef
2 cans chef boy-ardee pizza sauce with cheese
8 oz. grated cheddar cheese
8 oz. grated mozzarella
1 tsp. oregano
1/2 tsp. fennel seed
1 tbsp. cornstarch

Brown ground beef and drain. Add all other ingredients place in crock pot/crock
Pot and heat through. Serve with tortilla chips.

Potato Casserole

1 pkg frozen hash browns
1 small carton ranch dip
1 can cream of potato soup
Salt, pepper
Dried onions to taste
4-5 oz of grated cheddar cheese

Mix 1st 4 ingredients. Put into crock pot. Place grated cheese on top. Cook for 4 hours.

Potatoes Perfect

1/4 pound bacon, diced
2 med onions, thinly sliced
4 med potatoes, thinly sliced
1/2 pound cheddar cheese, thinly slice
Salt and pepper
Butter

Line crock pot with aluminum foil, leaving enough to overlap potatoes when finished.

Layer half each of the bacon, onions, potatoes and cheese in crock pot. Season to taste and dot with butter. Repeat layers of bacon, onions, potatoes and cheese. Dot with butter. Overlap with remaining foil. Cover and cook on low setting for 10 to 12 hours.

Provincial Chicken

1 1/2 pounds chicken tenders, frozen
2 small zucchini, diced
1 can (4 oz) sliced black olives
1 tablespoon sherry wine vinegar or balsamic vinegar
1 cans good-quality diced tomatoes (about 15 ounces)
1 cans (10 oz) cream of chicken soup with herbs
2 teaspoons dried parsley flakes
1 teaspoon dried basil
1 tablespoon dried minced onion
1 cup shredded cheddar cheese
2 to 3 tablespoons sour cream (optional)
Hot noodles, rice or pasta

Combine first 9 ingredients in 3 1/2-quart crock pot (or larger). Cover and cook on low for 6 to 8 hours. Add cheese and sour cream during the last 15 minutes. Serve over hot noodles, rice or pasta.

Pudding Cake

1 cup flour
1/2 cup sugar
1/2 cup coarsely chopped pecans, or walnuts
1/4 cup unsweetened cocoa
2 teaspoons baking powder
1/2 teaspoon salt
1/2 cup milk
1/4 cup oil
1 teaspoon vanilla extract
1 cup boiling water
1/2 cup chocolate syrup
Whipped cream or ice cream

Mix together first 6 ingredients in 6-cup mold. Stir in milk, oil and vanilla. Mix boiling water and chocolate syrup. Pour over batter. Place small trivet or band from canning jar in bottom of cooker, add 2 cups warm water. Place mold in cooker and cover with 4 layers of paper towels. Cover cooker and cook on high 3 to 4 hours. Serve warm with cream.

Pumpkin Bread

1 cup all-purpose flour
1 1/2 tsp baking powder
1 tsp pumpkin pie spice
1/2 cup brown sugar, firmly packed
2 tbsp vegetable oil
2 eggs
1/2 cup pumpkin (canned)
4 tbsp raisins or dried currants, finely chopped

In small bowl combine flour, baking powder and pumpkin pie spice; set aside. In med. mixing bowl combine brown sugar and oil; beat till well combined. Beat in eggs. Add pumpkin; mix well. Add flour mixture. Beat just until combined. Stir in raisins. Pour pumpkin mixture into 2 well-greased and floured 1/2-pint straight-sided canning jars. Cover jars tightly with greased foil. Place a piece of crumpled foil in 3-1/2 or 4 qt. crockery cooker with liner in place. Place jars atop crumpled foil. Cover; cook on high setting for 1-1/2 to 1-3/4 hours or until a wooden toothpick inserted near centers comes out clean.
Remove jars from cooker; cool 10 minutes in jars. Remove bread from jars. Cool thoroughly on wire rack. Makes 2 loaves.

Pumpkin Tea Bread

1/2 c. oil
1/2 c. sugar
1/2 c. brown sugar
2 beaten eggs
1 c. canned pumpkin
1 1/2 c. sifted flour
1/2 tsp. salt
1/2 tsp. cinnamon
1/2 tsp. nutmeg
1 tsp. soda
1 c. chopped walnuts

Blend oil and two sugars. Stir in beaten eggs and pumpkin. Sift dry ingredients together. Add and then stir in nuts. Pour batter into greased and floured 1 lb. 10oz. coffee can. Place can in crock pot. Cover top of can with 6-8 paper towels; place lid on top. Bake on high 2 1/2 - 3 1/2 hours.

Red Rice

4 to 6 slices bacon, fried & crumbled
1 large onion, coarsely chopped
2 cans chopped tomatoes, (15 oz each)
1 cup converted rice
1/2 to 1 cup cooked chopped ham
Salt and pepper, to taste
1/8 teaspoon hot pepper sauce, or to taste

Fry bacon; drain and crumble. Cook onion in bacon grease just until softened. Combine all ingredients in the crock pot. Cover and cook on low for 6 to 7 hours, or until rice is tender but not mushy.
Serves 6 to 8

Refried Bean Dip

1 (20 oz can) refried beans
1/4 teaspoon salt
1 cup shredded cheddar cheese
1 (4 oz can) chopped green chilies
2 tablespoons bottled taco sauce
1/2 cup chopped green onions
Tortilla chips

In crock pot combine beans with cheese, chilies, onions, salt, and taco sauce. Cover and cook on low for 2 to 2-1/2 hours. Serve hot from the pot.

Reuben Dip

1 small can sauerkraut
1 (8 oz.) cream cheese
1 (6 oz.) shredded Swiss cheese
6 ounces diced corned beef
2 tbsp. Thousand Island dressing

Drain and rinse sauerkraut, mix with cream cheese and Swiss cheese. Add diced corned beef and Thousand Island dressing. Cover and heat on low until cheeses are melted, stirring occasionally to blend all ingredients. Serve warm with crackers or cocktail rye bread.

Rhubarb Bake

1 3/4 cup fresh rhubarb
3/4 cup sugar
1 cinnamon stick
2 whole cloves
1 teaspoon grated lemon peel
1/4 cup butter or margarine
1/3 cup flour
1/3 cup sugar

Cut rhubarb into small pieces. Combine rhubarb with 3/4 cup sugar, cinnamon, cloves and lemon peel in cooker. Cover and cook on low for 3 to 4 hours. Remove whole spices. Spoon rhubarb into baking dish. Combine remaining ingredients and sprinkle over rhubarb. Bake at 400 degrees for 20 to 25 minutes.
Serves 4 to 6.

Rice Pudding

2 1/2 c. cooked rice
1 1/2 c. scalded milk
2/3 c. white or brown sugar
3 eggs, beaten
1 tsp. salt
2 tbsp. vanilla
1 tsp. cinnamon
1 tsp. nutmeg
1/2 c. raisins
3 tbsp. soft butter

Combine all ingredients. Pour into lightly greased crock pot. Cook on high 1 to 2 hours. Stir during first 30 minutes. Recipe can be doubled.

Rice Pudding With Fruit

1/2 gallon milk
1 cup uncooked rice
1 cup sugar
3 tablespoons cold margarine
1/4 teaspoon salt, optional
1 teaspoon vanilla extract
1/2 cup dried apricots or peaches, minced
1/4 teaspoon ground cinnamon

Use half nonfat and half whole milk or all nonfat for lower fat content. Can substitute evaporated milk for a very rich flavor. The cooking time will vary greatly, anywhere from 1 1/2 to 3 1/2 hours. The longer it cooks, the thicker it will be. It is important to have the dried apricots minced. Put all ingredients into the crock pot. Stir to blend well. Cover and cook on high for 1 1/2 hours; stir once after about an hour. Or, cook on high for the first 30 minutes, turn to low and cook as long as desired. Check after the first 2 hours of low cooking and stir. If the rice is not absorbing the milk quickly enough, turn the crock pot up to high again. Keep cover on at all times. Crock pot temperatures vary widely among different brands. Only experimentation can tell you the correct amount of time for cooking in your crock pot. Rarely will a crock pot recipe fail, though, as the long, slow cooking process does not require precise timing. Serves 8.

Rich Brownies In A Nut Crust

1/4 cup butter or margarine, melted
1 cup chopped nuts
1 family-size package brownie mix (about 23 oz.)

Pour melted butter into 2-pound coffee can; swirl to butter sides. Sprinkle with half the nuts. Mix brownies according to the package. Pour half the batter into coffee can, covering nuts evenly. Add remaining half of nuts, then batter. Place can in crock-pot. Cover top of can with 8 paper towels. Cover and bake on high setting for 3 hours. Do not check or remove cover until last hour. (If using bread 'n cake bake pan, bake in covered pan on high setting for 2 to 3 hours.) Remove can and discard paper towels. Let stand 5 minutes. Unmold and serve warm. 24 brownies (for 3 1/2-or 5-quart crock-pot).

Ricotta Amaretto Cheesecake

Crust:
1 cup vanilla wafer crumbs (about 21 to 23 cookies)
1 tablespoon sugar
1/8 teaspoon almond extract
3 tablespoons butter

Filling:
15 ounces light ricotta cheese
8 ounces cream cheese
2/3 cup sugar
3 large eggs plus 1 egg yolk
1/4 cup amaretto liqueur
2 tablespoons all-purpose flour
1/4 teaspoon almond extract

1/2 teaspoon vanilla extract

Combine crust ingredients well; pat into a 7-inch spring form pan. Beat sugar into the cheeses; add eggs; beat for 2 to 3 minutes on medium speed of an electric hand-held mixer. Add remaining filling ingredients and beat about 2 minutes more. Pour into prepared crust. Place the cheesecake on a rack in the crock pot (or use a "ring" of aluminum foil to keep it off the bottom of the pot). Cover and cook on high for 2 1/2 to 3 hours. Let stand in the covered pot (after turning it off) for about 1 to 2 hours, until cool enough to handle. Cool thoroughly before removing pan sides. Chill before serving; store leftovers in the refrigerator.

Roasted Veggie Trio Pot

3 cups (15 oz) sliced raw potatoes
3 cups sliced carrots
1-3/4 cups (one 15 oz can) Swanson beef broth
1/2 cup chopped onions

In a crock pot, combine potatoes, carrots and onion. Pour beef broth evenly over top. Cover and cook on high for 4 - 6 hours. Mix well before serving.

Reuben Casserole

1 (8 oz.) pkg. noodles, cooked
1 cans corned beef
3 1/2 c. sauerkraut
6 slices American cheese
16 oz. sour cream
1 (10 1/4 oz.) can cream of chicken soup
6 slices Swiss cheese

In a buttered quart crock pot, layer half the noodles, half the meat, all the sauerkraut, all the American cheese. Mix the sour cream and the chicken soup together and layer half of the soup mixture. Then layer the rest of the noodles, meat, soup mixture and then lastly the Swiss cheese. Cook on high for 2 hours, so that it bubbles well. Turn down to low for 1 or 2 hours. It helps to stir before serving, to mix the layers together some.

Russian Chicken

1 bottle Russian dressing (16 oz.)
1 envelope onion soup mix
1 jar apricot preserves (10 oz.)
4 pieces chicken -- (4 to 6)
Seasoned salt and pepper to taste

Combine dressing, preserves and onion soup mix in bowl and pour into a crock pot. Sprinkle chicken with seasoned salt and pepper. Place chicken, skin side down, in crock pot. Cook on low for 8 hours (high 4 hours) serves 4 - 6.

Salmon And Potato Casserole

4 potatoes, peeled and thinly sliced
3 tablespoons flour
Salt and pepper
1 can (16 ounces) salmon, drained and flaked
1 medium onion, chopped
1 cans (10 3/4 ounces) cream of mushroom soup
1/4 cup water
Nutmeg

Place half of the potatoes in greased crock pot. Sprinkle with half of the flour, salt and pepper. Cover with half the salmon; sprinkle with half the onion. Repeat layers in order. Combine soup and water. Pour over potato-salmon mixture. Dust with nutmeg. Cover and cook on low for 7-10 hours.
Serves 6.

Salmon Bake In Crockpot

3 cans salmon, 1 lb each
4 cups bread crumbs, soft 10 slices
1 cans tomatoes in puree, 1 lb.
1 green pepper, chopped
3 teaspoons lemon juice
1 can cream of onion soup, cond.
2 chicken bouillon cubes, crushed
6 eggs, well beaten
1 can cream of celery soup, cond.
1/2 cup milk

Grease removable liner well. Combine all ingredients, except celery soup and milk, in removable liner. Place liner in base. Cover and cook on low 4-6 hours or auto for 3 hours. Combine cream of celery soup with 1/2 cup of milk and heat in saucepan. Use as sauce for salmon bake.

Savory Salsa-Corn Cake

2 boxes corn muffin mix, (8 oz each)
1 cans creamed corn, (15 ounce)

2 eggs
1/2 cup sour cream
1 can chopped green chilies, (4 ounces) undrained
2 tablespoons soft margarine
3 to 4 tbs chunky salsa

In a medium bowl, combine creamed corn, eggs, sour cream, chilies, and margarine. Whisk together until well combined. Add corn muffin mix, stirring well to combine. Generously grease a 3 1/2-quart crock pot with margarine or butter. Pour batter into the crock pot. Spoon salsa over the top and cut into the batter. Cover and cook on high for about 2 1/2 hours. Turn heat off and let cool with lid ajar, for about 15 minutes. Loosen sides with a knife and invert onto a large plate. If a little of the top sticks to the bottom of the pot, dollop a little salsa on the top, or decorate with sour cream and chopped green onion. Serves 6 to 8.

Scalloped Corn

3 large eggs
1 cup half and half
1 tablespoon sugar
1/4 teaspoon salt
1/4 teaspoon pepper
3 to 4 tablespoons minced onion
2 cups frozen creamed corn, thawed
1 cup coarsely crushed cracker crumbs

Wisk milk and eggs together then mix in remaining ingredients. Pour into lightly buttered casserole which will fit in the crock pot. Cover and cook on high for 2 1/2 hours, or until knife inserted in center comes out clean. Serves 6 as a side dish.

Scalloped Potato-Tomato Pot

6 cups (20 oz) frozen shredded hash browns
2 cups (one 16 oz can) cut green beans, rinsed and drained
1/4 cup finely chopped onion
1 teaspoon dried parsley flakes
1 (10-3/4 oz) can healthy request cream of celery soup
1-3/4 cups (one 14-1/2 oz can) stewed tomatoes, undrained

In a crock pot, combine hash browns, green beans and onion. In a medium bowl, combine parsley flakes, celery soup and undrained stewed tomatoes. Add soup mixture to potato mixture. Mix well to combine. Cover and cook on low for 6 - 8 hours. Mix well before serving.

Scalloped Potatoes

10 large potatoes, thin slice
2 large onions, chopped
2 cans cheddar cheese soup, cond.
1 cup milk

In a small bowl, combine soup with milk. In removable liner, layer one half the potatoes and one half the chopped onions; spread one half the soup-milk mixtures. Repeat layering using rest of ingredients. Placed in base. Cover and cook on low for 6-8 hours, high for 3-4 hours or auto for 5 hours.

Scalloped Potatoes With Ham

1/2 cup diced ham
8 to 10 med. potatoes, thinly sliced
1 c. grated American cheese
Salt and pepper
1 can cream of mushroom soup, or 1 cup medium white sauce
Paprika
1 onion, thinly sliced

In crock pot layer half of ham, half of potatoes, half of onions, half of cheese. Sprinkle with salt and pepper. Repeat layers with remaining half of ingredients. Spoon undiluted soup or white sauce over top and sprinkle with paprika. Cover and cook on low for 7 to 9 hours.

Shrimp Creole

1 1/2 c diced celery
1 1/4 c chopped onion
3/4 c chopped bell pepper
1 (8oz) can tomato sauce
1 (28 oz) can whole tomatoes
1 clove garlic
1 tsp salt
1/4 tsp pepper
6 drops Tabasco sauce (optional)
1 lb shrimp, deveined and shelled

Combine all ingredients except shrimp. Cook 3 - 4 hours on high or 6 - 8 hours on low. Add shrimp last hour of cooking. Serve over hot rice. Chicken, rabbit or crawfish may be substituted for the shrimp. * 1 tsp garlic salt or 1/4 tsp garlic powder may be substituted.

Shrimp Marinara

1 (16 oz.) can of tomatoes, cut up
2 tbsp. minced parsley
1 clove of garlic, minced
1/2 tsp. dried basil
1 tsp. salt
1/4 tsp. pepper
1 tsp. dried oregano
1 (6 oz.) can tomato paste
1/2 tsp. seasoned salt
1 lb. cooked shelled shrimp
Grated parmesan cheese
Cooked spaghetti

In a crock pot, combine tomatoes with parsley, garlic, basil, salt, pepper, oregano, tomato paste and seasoned salt. Cover and cook on low for 6 to 7 hours. Turn control to high, stir in shrimp, cover and cook on high for 10 to 15 minutes more. Serve over cooked spaghetti. Top with parmesan cheese.

Simple Saucy Potatoes

4 cans (15 ounces each) sliced white potatoes, drained
2 cans condensed cream of celery soup, undiluted
2 cups sour cream
10 bacon strips, cooked and crumbled
6 green onions, thinly sliced

Place potatoes in crock pot. Combine the remaining ingredients; pour over the potatoes and mix well. Cover and cook on high for 4-5 hours.

Slow-Cooked Broccoli

2 packages (10 oz. each) frozen chopped broccoli, partially thawed
1 can (10-3/4 oz.) condensed cream of celery soup, undiluted
1-1/2 cups shredded sharp cheddar cheese, divided
1/4 cup chopped onion
1/2 teaspoon Worcestershire sauce
1/4 teaspoon pepper
1 cup crushed butter-flavored crackers (about 25)
2 tablespoons butter or margarine

In a large bowl, combine broccoli, soup, 1 cup cheese, onion, Worcestershire sauce and pepper.

Pour into a greased crock pot. Sprinkle crackers on top; dot with butter. Cover and cook on high for 2-1/2 to 3 hours. Sprinkle with remaining cheese. Cook 10 minutes longer or until the cheese is melted. Makes 8-10 servings.

Slow Cooked Corn Pudding

1/4 cup chopped onion
1/4 cup chopped green pepper
1/4 cup chopped fresh tomato
1 16 oz can cream-style corn
4 large eggs
1/2 cup evaporated milk
1/2 teaspoon salt
1/4 teaspoon pepper

Sauté onion and green pepper until slightly softened; add tomato and sauté for 1 minute more. In a medium-sized bowl, whisk together the eggs, milk, creamed corn and seasonings; add the sautéed vegetables. lightly grease a 3 1/2 quart crock pot (or a soufflé dish which fits in a larger crock pot) and pour the mixture in. cook on high 2 1/2 to 3 hours; add grated cheese to the top and cook until cheese is melted.

Slow Cooker Candy

2 lbs. white almond bark
4 oz. bar German chocolate
12 oz. pkg. semi-sweet chocolate chips
24 oz. jar dry roasted peanuts

Put all ingredients in crock pot; cook 1 hour on high. Do not stir. Turn crock pot to low and stir every 15 minutes for 1 hour. Drop on waxed paper and cool. Store in an air-tight container.

Slow Cooker Creamy Corn

1 large bag frozen corn
8 ounces pkg. cream cheese
1 stick margarine
Salt and pepper to taste

Melt cream cheese and margarine in microwave. Spray crock pot with vegetable spray. Put melted cream cheese and margarine in crock pot. Add corn, salt and pepper. Cook in crock pot for two hours on low.

Slow Cooker Creamy Scalloped Potatoes And Ham

3 lbs. med. size potatoes peeled and sliced
1 onion chopped
1 cup shredded cheddar cheese
1 cup cooked ham
1 can (10 3/4 oz) reduced fat cream of mushroom soup
1/2 cup water

Combine potatoes, onion, cheese and ham in crock pot. In small bowl, stir together soup & water. Pour over potato mixture. Cover pot. Cook on high for 4 hours or until potatoes are tender. Stir mixture just before serving. Makes 6 servings

Slow Cooker Seafood Chowder

2 lbs. frozen fish filets
1/4 lb. bacon or salt pork, diced
1 medium onion, chopped
4 medium potatoes, peeled and cubed
2 cups water
1 1/2 tsp. salt (unless you are using fresh salt-water fish)
1/4 tsp. pepper
1 can evaporated milk

Thaw frozen fish in refrigerator. Cut into bite-sized pieces. In skillet, sauté bacon or salt pork and onion until meat is cooked and onion is golden. Drain and put into crock pot with the fish pieces. Add potatoes, water, salt and pepper. Cover and cook on low for 6 - 9 hours. Add evaporated milk during last hour. If the chowder is thicker than you like, add more milk (any kind).

Slow Cooker Shrimp Creole

1 1/2 c. diced celery
1 1/4 c. chopped onion
3/4 c. chopped bell pepper
1 (8 oz.) can tomato sauce
1 (28 oz.) can whole tomatoes
1 clove garlic
1 tsp. salt

1/4 tsp. pepper
6 drops Tabasco (opt.)
1 lb. shrimp, deveined & shelled
1 teaspoon garlic salt or 1/4 teaspoon garlic powder.

Combine all ingredients except shrimp. Cook 3 to 4 hours on high or 6 to 8 hours on low. Add shrimp last hour of cooking. Serve over hot rice. Chicken, rabbit or crawfish may be substituted for shrimp. Stove top version, if you don't have a crock pot. Sauté celery, onion and bell peppers in oil or butter until tender. Add remaining ingredients except meat being used. Simmer at least 30 minutes to an hour. Add shrimp or whatever meat you wish and simmer 30 minutes more.

Southern Style Green Bean & Potato Casserole

4 to 6 medium red potatoes, sliced about 1/4" thick (peeled or not)
4 to 5 cups whole fresh green beans, trimmed
6 slices bacon, diced fried and drained
2 tablespoons minced dried onion
1 cans 98% fat free cream of celery soup
Salt and pepper to taste

Place sliced potatoes and green beans in crock pot; add other ingredients. Cover and cook on low 7 to 9 hours. Serves 4 to 6.

Sour Cream Chili Bake

1 pound ground beef
1 can pinto beans, drained (15 oz)
1 cans enchilada sauce (10 oz)
1 cans tomato sauce (8 oz)
1 cup shredded process American cheese
1 tablespoon instant minced onion
1 cup water
4 cups corn chips
1 cup sour cream
1/2 cup shredded process American cheese

Brown ground beef; drain. Transfer meat to crock pot. Stir in beans, enchilada sauce, and tomato
Sauce, 1 cup of cheese, onion and 1 cup of water. Reserve 1 cup of corn chips; crush the remaining chips and add to the meat mixture. Cover and cook on low heat for 8 to 10 hours. To serve, top with sour cream, remaining cheese, and reserved corn chips.

Spaghetti Sauce With Chicken & Sausage

1 lb. Italian sausage
3-4 boneless chicken breasts cut into 1-inch chunks
1 cup chopped green pepper
1 cup chopped onion
1-2 tsp. Italian seasoning
2 (4 oz. each) cans mushroom stems and pieces, drained
2 jars favorite spaghetti sauce
Hot cooked pasta

In skillet, brown Italian sausage, piercing casings to allow excess fat to run out. Remove to plate and cut into 1/2 to 1-inch chunks. In same skillet, brown chicken pieces. Place sausage and chicken in crock pot. Add pepper and onion. Sprinkle with Italian seasoning. Add mushrooms. Pour sauce over everything. Cover and cook on low for 6 to 8 hours. Stir before serving over spaghetti or other pasta.

Spaghetti Squash

2 cups water
1 spaghetti squash, a size which will fit in crock pot

With a skewer or large fork, puncture several holes in the squash. Pour water in the crock pot, add the whole squash. Cover and cook on low for 8 to 9 hours. Split and remove seeds, then transfer the "spaghetti" strands to a bowl. Serve tossed with butter and salt and pepper, parmesan cheese or your favorite sauce.

Spanish Chicken

2 lb. boneless skinless chicken breast
Seasoned salt & pepper to taste
Black olives, pitted
Sliced mushrooms, drained
Stewed tomatoes
Liquid to cover (beer, tomato soup or tomato sauce w/equal amount of water or stock)
Cut chicken into bite-sized pieces; season. Place with remaining ingredients in crock pot. Simmer all day on low. Serve over rice. Serves 4.

Spicy Chicken Wings

3 tbsp. vinegar
24 chicken wings, drumsticks
1/4 c. hot pepper sauce or less

1/2 c. melted butter
1 pkg. hidden valley ranch original dry salad dressing mix

Preheat oven to 350 degrees. Mix all ingredients together except chicken wings and salad dressing mix. Place chicken wings in baking dish or pan in a single layer. Pour mixture over wings. Sprinkle with dry dressing mix. Bake 25 - 30 minutes or until browned. Sprinkle with paprika if you like. Chicken wings may be made in crock pot - cook on low 4 to 5 hours.

Spicy Franks

1 cup ketchup
1/4 cup brown sugar, packed
1 tablespoon red wine vinegar
2 teaspoons soy sauce
2 teaspoons Dijon mustard
1/8 teaspoon garlic powder
1 pound hot dogs, cut into bite-size pieces, or cocktail wieners, smoked sausage, etc.

Combine everything but hot dogs in the crock pot; cover and cook on high 1 to 2 hours, until well blended. Add hot dogs, stir, and cook another 1 to 2 hours, until heated through. Turn to low to keep warm and serve from the crock pot.

Spicy Marmalade Meatballs

Meatballs:
2 lbs ground beef (chuck)
1/2 cup bread crumbs
1 teaspoon Worcestershire sauce
1/2 teaspoon salt
1/4 teaspoon pepper
1 small onion, minced
1/2 teaspoon chili powder
1/4 teaspoon garlic powder
3 eggs

Sauce:
2 cups ketchup
1/4 cup Worcestershire sauce
1 jar orange marmalade (10 to 12 ounces)
Dash cayenne, more or less to taste
1 teaspoon chili powder

Combine sauce ingredients in crock pot; cover and cook on high while preparing meatballs. Combine meatball ingredients. Heat a large skillet over medium high heat. Add meatballs; brown on all sides. You might have to do this in batches. Place browned meatballs in a 325° oven and bake for 45 minutes (if the skillet isn't ovenproof, transfer to a baking dish). Transfer meatballs to crock pot with a slotted spoon or drain on brown paper first. Cover and reduce to low for 2 to 4 hours. Serve hot as an appetizer or over rice for a main dish. Makes 24 to 48 meatballs, depending on size.

Spicy Refried Bean Dip

2 cans refried beans, (16ounce each)
1 package taco seasoning mix, about 1 1/4 oz
1/2 cup chopped onion
2 cups Monterey jack cheese, shredded
Tabasco sauce, to taste
Chopped jalapeno or mild chilies, to taste

Place refried beans, taco seasoning, onion, cheese, and Tabasco sauce in the crock pot; stir well. Stir in chopped chilies. Cover and cook on low until cheese is melted, about 1 hour; add a little water if mixture seems too thick. Serve from the crock pot with French bread, crackers, or chips. Makes about 4 cups.

Spinach, Cheese & Bacon Strata

4 cups sliced & buttered French bread, cubed
1 bag frozen spinach (16 oz)
6 to 8 ounces diced, cooked bacon, ham, or turkey ham
1 1/2 to 2 cups shredded cheddar cheese
Salt and pepper, to taste
1 can (10oz) cream of mushroom soup (the 98% fat free is fine)
1/2 cup evaporated milk
5 eggs
1 tablespoon minced dried onion (optional)

Lightly butter a 3 1/2-quart crock pot. Layer with half of the buttered bread cubes, spinach, bacon, and cheese; salt and pepper to taste. Repeat layers ending with cheese. Whisk together the soup, milk, eggs, and dried onion. Pour over crock pot mixture. Chill for 1 hour or overnight. Cover and cook on low for 3 1/2 to 4 1/2 hours. Serves 4 to 6.

Spinach Soufflé

2 pounds frozen spinach, thawed and drained
1/4 cup grated onion
1 8 oz pkg light cream cheese, softened
1/2 cup mayonnaise
1/2 cup shredded cheddar cheese
2 eggs, beaten
1/4 teaspoon white or black pepper
Dash nutmeg

Mix thawed and drained spinach together with onion. Beat remaining ingredients and blend in spinach mixture. Spoon mixture into a lightly buttered 3 1/2-quart crock pot (or soufflé dish to fit in a larger crock pot) and cook on high for 2 to 3 hours.

Split Pea Soup

1 (16 oz.) pkg. dried green split peas, rinsed
1 hambone, or 2 meaty ham hocks, or 2 c. diced ham
3 carrots, peeled & sliced
1 med. onion, chopped
2 stalks of celery plus leaves, chopped
1 or 2 cloves of garlic, minced
1 bay leaf1/4 c. fresh parsley, chopped (optional)
1 tbsp. seasoned salt (or to taste)
1/2 tsp. fresh pepper
1 1/2 qts. Hot water

Layer ingredients in crock pot, pour in water. Do not stir. Cover and cook on high 4 to 5 hours or on low 8 to 10 hours until peas are very soft and ham falls off bone. Remove bones and bay leaf. Serve garnished with croutons.

Spoon Peaches

1/3 cup sugar
1/2 cup brown sugar
2 tsp. margarine, melted
1/2 can evaporated milk
3/4 cup bisquik
2 eggs
2 cups peaches, mashed
2 tsp. vanilla
3/4 tsp. cinnamon

Spray crock pot with non-stick cooking spray. Combine sugars and bisquik. Add eggs and vanilla. Add margarine and milk. Add peaches and cinnamon. Pour into crock pot. Cook on low for 6 to 8 hours.

Squash Casserole I

5 cups yellow squash, canned or frozen
1/2 cup butter or margarine, melted
1 can cream of chicken soup
2 slices cubed bread
1 cup sour cream

Place squash in crock pot with butter and cook for 1 hour. Add soup as it comes from the can, and cook until hot. Add bread and sour cream and cook until bubbly.

Squash Casserole II

2 pounds yellow summer squash or zucchini, thinly sliced (about 6 cups)
1/2 medium onion, chopped
1 cup pared shredded carrot
1 cans (10 1/4 ounces) condensed cream of chicken soup
1 cup sour cream
1/4 cup flour
1 package (8 ounces) seasoned stuffing crumbs
1/2 cup butter or margarine, melted

In large bowl, combine squash, onion, carrot and soup. Mix sour cream and flour, stir into vegetables. Toss stuffing crumbs with butter and place half in crock pot. Add vegetable mixture and top with remaining stuffing crumbs. Cover and cook on low for 6-8 hrs. Serves 4 to 6.

Stewed Tomatoes

6 to 8 ripe tomatoes
2 tablespoons margarine
1 medium onion, thinly sliced
3/4 cup chopped celery
1/2 cup chopped green pepper
3 tablespoons sugar (more or less)
1 small bay leaf
1 teaspoon salt
1/8 teaspoon pepper

Core tomatoes; place in boiling water for about 15 to 20 seconds, then into ice water to cool quickly; peel. Cut tomatoes in wedges. In crock pot, combine all ingredients. Cover and cook on low 8-9 hours. Remove bay leaf. Sprinkle top with parsley, if desired. Serve as a side dish or freeze in portions for soups or other recipes. Serves 6.

Streusel Pound Cake

1 pkg. pound cake mix (16 oz.) size
1/4 c. packed brown sugar
1 tbsp. flour
1/4 c. finely chopped nuts
1 tsp. cinnamon

Mix cake mix according to package. Pour batter into well greased and
Floured 2 pound coffee tin. Combine sugar, flour, nuts and cinnamon and sprinkle over cake batter. Place can in Crockpot. Cover top of can with 8 layers of paper towels. Cover pot and bake on high 3 to 4 hours.

Stuffed Green Peppers

1 package (10 oz) frozen corn kernels
1 can (15 oz) red kidney beans drained and rinsed
1 can (14.5 oz) diced tomatoes
1/4 cup salsa
1/4 cup chopped onions
1 1/2 cups cooked rice
1 tsp Worcestershire sauce
1/4 tsp salt
1/2 tsp pepper
2 cups shredded reduced fat cheddar cheese, divided
6 green peppers. Tops removed & seeded

Combine all ingredients, except 1/4 cup cheese and green peppers. Stuff peppers. Arrange peppers in crock pot. Cover, cook on low 6 - 8 hours (high 3 - 4 hours) sprinkle with 1/4 cup cheese during the last 30 minutes. Makes 6 servings

Stuffed Potatoes

6 baking potatoes, washed
3 tbsp butter
1 cup milk
Chopped chives

1 tsp salt
1//8 tsp pepper
3 tbsp parmesan cheese
Shredded cheddar cheese

Place damp potatoes in bottom of cooker. Cover and cook on low for 6 to 8 hours. Remove and cut a slice, lengthwise, from each potato. Scoop out insides. Save shell. Add remaining ingredients and beat until fluffy. Spoon mixture back into shells and top each with shredded cheddar cheese. Bake at 425 degrees for 15 minutes or until cheese is melted and bubbly. Serves 6.

Sugared Pecans

16 ounces pecan halves
1/2 cup butter, melted
1/2 cup powdered sugar
1 1/2 teaspoons ground cinnamon
1/4 teaspoon ground ginger
1/4 teaspoon ground allspice

Stir the pecans and butter in a 3 1/2-quart crock pot until combined. Add powdered sugar, stirring to coat. Cover and cook on high for 15 minutes. Turn to low and cook uncovered for about 2 hours, or until the nuts are covered with a crisp glaze. Transfer to a bowl, combine spices and sift over nuts, tossing to distribute evenly. Cool before serving.

Sugared Walnuts & Pecans

1 pound pecans or walnut pieces
1/2 cup unsalted butter - melted
1/2 cup powdered sugar
1/4 tsp allspice - ground
1/8 tsp cloves - ground
1 1/2 tsp cinnamon - ground
1/4 tsp ginger - ground

Preheat crock pot on high for 15 minutes. First, in preheated crock pot stir the walnuts (or pecans) and butter until mixed well. Add the powdered sugar, stirring to coat evenly. Cover and slow-cook on high for 15 minutes. Reduce the heat to low and slow cook, uncovered, stirring occasionally, until the nuts are coated with a crisp glaze (should be about 2 hours.) transfer the nuts to a bowl. In another small bowl, combine the spices and sift them over the nuts, stirring to coat evenly. Let cool before serving.

Sun-Dried Tomato Spaghetti Sauce

1 1/2 cups chopped sun-dried tomatoes
1 medium onion, chopped
1 cup celery, chopped
2 cloves garlic, minced
36 oz whole or chopped tomatoes, undrained
2/3 cup Chablis or other dry white wine 1
Teaspoon dried fennel seed
1 1/2 tsp. basil
1/2 teaspoon oregano
1/2 teaspoon pepper
Salt to taste

Place all ingredients in crock pot and cook on low for 6-8 hours. Note: you can add mushrooms if desired.

Sunshine Squash

1 butternut squash, about 2 pounds, peeled, seeded and diced
1 can (14-1/2-ounce) tomatoes, undrained
1 can (about 15-ounces) corn, drained
1 medium onion, coarsely chopped
1 clove garlic, minced well
1 green bell pepper, seeded and cut into 1-" pieces
1 canned green chili, coarsely chopped
1/2 cup chicken broth
1/2 teaspoon salt
1/4 teaspoon black pepper
1 tablespoon plus 1-1/2- teaspoons tomato paste

Combine all ingredients except tomato paste in slow-cooker. Cover and cook on low 6 hours or until squash is tender. Remove about 1/4- cup cooking liquid and blend with tomato paste. Stir into slow-cooker. Cook 30 minutes or until mixture is slightly thickened and heated through. Serves 6-8.

Sweet And Sour Cabbage

4 bacon slices, diced
1/4 cup packed
Brown sugar
2 tbsp. all-purpose flour
1/2 tsp. salt

1/8 tsp. pepper
1/4 cup water
1/4 cup vinegar
1 medium head red cabbage, shredded (about 8 cups)
1 small onion finely chopped

In a skillet, cook bacon until crisp; reserve drippings. Combine 1 tbsp. drippings in a crock pot with remaining ingredients, except cooked bacon. Cover and cook on low 6 1/2 to 7 hours or until cabbage is tender. Spoon into serving bowl; sprinkle with reserved bacon.

Sweet 'N' Sour Chicken

6 med. carrots cut into 1/2" chunks
1/2 c. finely chopped green pepper
1 sm. onion, finely chopped
3 split chicken breasts (remove skin, optional)
1/2 tsp. salt
1 (10 oz.) jar sweet n sour sauce
1 (15 oz.) can pineapple chunks, drained
2 tbsp. cornstarch

Place all ingredients in crock pot with chicken on top. Cover and cook on low 6-8 hours. Remove chicken and thicken with 2 tablespoons cornstarch dissolved to a medium thick paste with water. Pour over chicken breasts - or remove chicken from bone and come with sauce mixture. Serve with steamed white or brown rice.

Sweet And Sour Franks

1 cup chili sauce
1 cup currant jelly
3 tablespoons lemon juice
1 tablespoon prepared mustard
2 pounds cocktail franks or hot dogs cut into bite-sized pieces
2 cans pineapple chunks, 27 ozs

Combine first four ingredients in crock pot; mix well to break up jelly chunks. Cover and cook on high 15 to 20 minutes to soften jelly and blend sauce ingredients. Add cut-up hot dogs or cocktail franks. Add pineapple. Cover and cook on high for 2 hours; or low for 4 hours. Keep on low while serving.

Sweet And Sour Kielbasa

1 pound kielbasa
1 (10 oz.) jar red currant jelly
1/2 (5 oz.) jar golden spicy mustard (add whole jar for more spicy)

Cut kielbasa to bite-size pieces. Add to boiling water. Boil 8 to 10 minutes; poke with fork to release grease from meat. In crock pot, melt jelly on low heat. Add mustard. When kielbasa is done boiling, rinse, and then adds to crock pot mixture. Coat all of the meat. Simmer for 1 hour or more on low.

Sweet And Sour Sausage Balls

1/2 c. brown sugar
2 lbs. sausage
1 1/4 c. ketchup
1 tbsp. soy sauce
1 tbsp. lemon juice
1 can chunk pineapple

Roll sausage in balls, brown and add other ingredients. Cook until done in crock pot.

Sweet And Sour Shrimp

1 package (6 ox.) frozen Chinese pea pods, partially thawed
1 can (13 oz.) juice-pack pineapple chunks or tidbits (drain and reserve juice)
2 tbsp cornstarch
3 tbsp sugar
1 chicken bouillon cube
1 cup boiling water
1/2 cup reserved pineapple juice
2 tsp soy sauce
1/2 tsp ground ginger
2 cans (4 1/2 oz. each) shrimp, rinsed & drained
2 tbsp cider vinegar
Fluffy rice

Place pea pods and drained pineapple in crock-pot. In a small saucepan, stir together cornstarch and sugar. Dissolve bouillon cube in boiling water and add with juice, soy sauce and ginger to saucepan. Bring to a boil, stirring, and cook sauce for about 1 minute or until thickened and transparent. Gently blend sauce into pea pods and pineapple. Cover and cook on low setting for 4 to 6 hours. Before serving, add shrimp and vinegar, stirring carefully to avoid breaking up shrimp. Serve over hot rice. 4 to 5 servings (about 1 1/2 quarts)

Sweet Potato And Pineapple Pudding

3 pounds sweet potatoes, peeled and shredded
2 cans (8 oz.) crushed pineapple in unsweetened juice, undrained
1 cans (12 oz.) evaporated milk
1 1/4 cups brown sugar, firmly packed
6 t. margarine or butter cut in cubes
3 eggs, slightly beaten
1 t. ground cinnamon
1/2 t. nutmeg

Lightly grease crock pot. In crock pot, combine sweet potatoes, pineapple, evaporated milk, brown sugar, margarine, eggs, cinnamon, and nutmeg. Cover and cook on low 7-8 hours or on high 4 hours, stirring every 2 hours until the potatoes are tender. Serve hot or at room temperature. Note: this dish may appear to be curdling; however it will come together toward the end of the cooking. Serve 10 -12. (This was for the 5 quart model).

Sweet Potatoes With Apples

5 medium sweet potatoes
3 apples (such as granny smith) peeled & cored, cut in wedges
1/4 teaspoon ground nutmeg
1/4 teaspoon ground cinnamon
1/4 cup maple flavored syrup
2 tablespoons butter, melted
1/4 cup pecan pieces

Generously grease the bottom and sides of the crock pot with butter or margarine. Peel sweet potatoes; cut into 1/2" slices. Place on bottom of crock pot. Top with apple wedges; then nutmeg and cinnamon, maple syrup, and the melted butter. Cover and cook on low about 4 hours or until potatoes are tender. Sprinkle with pecans the last 30 minutes. Serves 4 to 6.

Sweet Sweet-Potatoes

2 pounds sweet potatoes---peel and grated
1/3 cup brown sugar---packed good
1/4 cup butter---melted
1/4 cup coconut---flaked
1/4 cup broken pecans---toasted
1/4 teaspoon cinnamon
1/4 teaspoon coconut extract
1/4 teaspoon vanilla

In a crock pot, combine potatoes, sugar, butter, coconut, pecans and cinnamon. Cover and cook on low for 6-8 hours or on high for 3-4 hours. Stir in coconut and vanilla extracts.

Swiss Cheese Scalloped Potatoes

2 pounds baking potatoes, peeled and thinly sliced
1/2 cup finely chopped yellow onion
1/4 tsp salt
1/4 tsp ground nutmeg
3 tbs butter, cut into 1/8-inch pieces
1/2 cup milk
2 tbs all-purpose flour
3 oz. Swiss cheese slices, torn into small pieces
1/4 cup finely chopped green onion (optional)

Layer half the potatoes, 1/4 cup onion, 1/8 tsp salt, 1/8 tsp nutmeg, 1 tbs butter in crock pot. Repeat layers. Cover and cook on low 7 hours or on high 4 hours. Remove potatoes with slotted spoon to serving dish. Blend milk and flour in small bowl until smooth. Stir mixture into crock pot. Add cheese; stir to combine. If crock pot is on low, turn to high, cover and cook until slightly thickened, about 10 minutes. Stir. Pour cheese mixture over potatoes and serve. Garnish with chopped green onions, if desired. Makes 5 to 6 servings.

Swiss Chicken Casserole

6 chicken breasts, boneless and skinless
6 slices Swiss cheese
1 can cream of mushroom soup
1/4 cup milk
2 cups stuffing mix
1/2 cup butter or margarine, melted

Lightly grease crock pot or spray with cooking spray. Place chicken breasts in pot. Top with cheese. Combine soup and milk, stirring well. Spoon over cheese; sprinkle with stuffing mix. Drizzle melted butter over stuffing mix. Cook on low 8 to 10 hours or high 4 to 6 hours. Serves 6.

Taco Chili

1 1/2 to 2 pounds lean ground beef
1 medium onion, chopped
1 pkg (1 1/4oz) taco seasoning mix

2 cans (14 1/2oz ea.) diced tomatoes

1 can (10oz) diced tomatoes with green chilies
1 cans (16oz) pinto beans, rinsed and drained
1 15oz can chili beans in sauce
1 cup frozen whole kernel corn
Shredded cheese (mozzarella, Monterey jack or
Cheddar)
Slightly crushed tortilla chips

In a large skillet, cook ground beef and onion, one-half at a time, till meat is browned and onion is tender. Drain off fat. Transfer to a 3 1/2- to 5-quart crockery cooker. Stir in dry taco seasoning mix, diced tomatoes, diced tomatoes with green chilies, pinto beans, chili beans in chili sauce, and corn. Cover; cook on low for 8 to 10 hours or on high for 4 to 5 hours. Sprinkle each serving with some cheese and chips. Makes 8 servings.

Texas Chili

6 strips bacon
2 lbs. boneless beef cubes
2 cans (15 oz.) kidney beans, drained
1 can (28 oz.) tomatoes, cut up
1 cans (8 oz.) tomato sauce
1 c. finely chopped onion
1/2 c. thinly sliced carrots
1/2 c. finely chopped green pepper
1/2 c. finely chopped celery
2 tbsp. minced parsley
2 cloves garlic minced
1 bay leaf
2 tbsp. chili powder
1 tsp. salt
1/8 tsp. pepper

Fry bacon until crisp. Remove bacon and drain on paper towel. Brown half the beef cubes in pan with bacon drippings five minutes. Place in crock pot. Repeat with remaining meat. Stir bacon and remaining ingredients into 3 1/2 quart crock pot. Cover and cook on low setting about 10 hours or until beef is tender. Stir occasionally. If you don't have a crock pot place in large pot, cover, place on stove under low heat and follow above.

Teriyaki Sauce Wings

3 pounds chicken wings
1 onion, chopped
1 cup soy sauce
1 cup brown sugar
2 teaspoons ground ginger
2 cloves garlic, crushed
1/4 cup dry sherry

Rinse chicken, and pat dry. Cut off wing tips and discard. Cut each wing into 2 pieces, cutting at the joint. Broil wings 4 inches from heat for about 10 minutes on each side, or until browned. Transfer to crock pot. Mix all remaining ingredients together and pour over chicken wings. Cook, covered, on low for 5 to 6 hours or on high for 2 to 3 hours. Stir once or twice to keep wings coated with sauce. Makes about 32 wings.

Triple Chocolate Mess

1 package chocolate cake mix (any)
1 pint sour cream
1 pkg. instant chocolate pudding (any size)
1 6oz. bag chocolate chips
3/4 c. oil
4 eggs
1 c. water

Spray crock pot with non-stick spray. Mix all ingredients. Cook on low for 6-8 hours try not to lift the lid. Serve with ice cream.

Tuna Noodle Casserole

2 cans cream of celery soup
1/3 cup dry sherry
2/3 cup milk
2 tablespoons parsley flakes
10 ounces frozen peas
2 cans tuna, drained
10 ounces egg noodles, cooked
2 tablespoons butter or margarine
Dash curry powder (optional)

In a large bowl, thoroughly combine soup, sherry, milk, parsley flakes, vegetables, and tuna. Fold in noodles. Pour into greased crock pot. Dot with butter or margarine. Cover and cook on low 7 to 9 hours. (Cook noodles just until tender.)

Tuna Salad Casserole

2 cans tuna, drained and flaked
1 can cream of celery soup
4 hard-cooked eggs, chopped
1 cup diced celery
1/2 cup mayonnaise
1/4 tsp. pepper
1 1/2 cups crushed potato chips

Combine all ingredients except 1/4 cup of the crushed potato chips; stir well. Pour into greased crock pot. Top with remaining potato chips. Cover and cook on low setting for 5-8 hours.

Turkey And Rice Casserole

2 cans cream of mushroom soup
3 cups water
3 cups converted long-grain white rice (uncooked)
1 cup thinly sliced celery
1 to 2 cups cubed cooked turkey
2 cups frozen mixed vegetables (peas & carrots, oriental mix, etc.)
1 teaspoon poultry seasoning
1 tablespoon dried minced onion

Pour soup and water into crock pot and stir to combine. Add remaining ingredients and mix well. Cover and cook 6 to 8 hours on low or 3 to 4 hours on high. Add soy sauce if desired.

Turkey Barbecue

2 to 3 lb. turkey fillets
2 green peppers
1 teaspoon. Celery salt
Dash of pepper
2 teaspoon. Chopped onion
18 ounce thick barbecue sauce

Prepare turkey fillets with dash of pepper across tops. Bake in 350 degree oven for 1 hour covered. Uncover for desired darker color. Prepare chopped green peppers, onions. Mix barbecue sauce, celery salt, (thin with water if needed) in 5 quart crock pot, set on high. Add green peppers and onions. Allow to heat while turkey is baking. Chop turkey (as desired in small to medium chunks) and add to crock pot. Simmer for 2 to 3 hours, or turn to low and cook for 4 to 6 hours. Serve on fresh rolls. Serves 4 to 6.

Turkey Madeira

1 1/2 lb turkey breast tenders
2 ounce porcini mushrooms (dried)
3/4 cup chicken broth
3 tablespoons Madeira wine
1 tablespoon lemon juice
Salt and pepper to taste

Cover and cook on low for 6 to 8 hours. Thicken juices with cornstarch if desired, and serve with rice. Serves 4.

Vegetable Beef Soup

1 pound ground chuck
1 cup chopped onion
1 large (28 oz.) can whole tomatoes (chopped)
3 cup diced potatoes
1 (16 oz.) can cut green beans
2 teaspoon chili powder
2-3 dashes cayenne pepper sauce
2 (10 1/2 oz.) cans condensed beef bouillon
1 cup chopped celery
1 cup sliced carrots
1 teaspoon salt
1 teaspoon Worcestershire sauce

Brown meat with onion and celery; drain off fat. Stir in remaining ingredients and add 1 or 2 cups water. Cover and cook on low for 8-10 hours.

Vegetable Casserole

2 cups carrots, cut in strips, cooked & drained
2 cups celery, diced
1 onion, diced
1/4 cup green pepper, diced
1 pint tomato juice
4 cups green beans, drained

1 teaspoon salt
Dash of pepper
3 tablespoons tapioca
1 tablespoon sugar

Mix all ingredients together in crock pot. Dot with 2 tablespoons margarine and cook on low for 8-10 hour or on high for 4-5 hours.

Vegetable Curry

4 medium carrots, bias sliced into inch slices
2 medium potatoes, cut into 1/2 cubes
15 ounces can garbanzo beans, drained
8 ounces green beans cut into 1 piece
1 cup coarsely chopped onion
3 to 4 cloves garlic, minced
2 tablespoons quick-cooking tapioca
2 teaspoons curry powder
1 teaspoon ground coriander
1/2 teaspoon crushed red pepper
1/4 teaspoon salt
1/8 teaspoon ground cinnamon
14 ounces can vegetable broth
16 ounces can tomatoes, cut up
2 cups hot cooked rice

in a 3 1/2, 4, or 5 quart crockery cooker combine carrots, garbanzo beans, potatoes, green beans, onion, garlic, tapioca, curry powder, coriander, red pepper (if desired), salt, and cinnamon. Pour broth over all. Cover; cook on low-heat setting for 8 to 10 hours or on high-heat setting for 4 to 5 hours. Stir in undrained tomatoes. Cover; let stand 5 minutes. Serve with cooked rice. Makes 4 servings.

Vegetable Pasta For Crockpot

2 tablespoons butter or margarine
1 zucchini, 1/4" slice
1 yellow squash, 1/4" slice
2 carrots, thinly sliced
1 1/2 cups mushrooms, fresh, sliced
1 package broccoli, frozen, cuts
4 green onions, sliced
2 to 3 cloves garlic, minced

1/2 teaspoon basil, dried
1/4 teaspoon salt
1/2 teaspoon pepper
1 cup parmesan cheese, grated
12 ounces fettuccine
1 cup mozzarella cheese, shredded
1 cup cream
2 egg yolks

Rub crock wall with butter. Put zucchini, yellow squash, carrots, mushrooms, broccoli, onions, garlic, seasonings and parmesan in the crock pot. Cover; cook on high 2 hours. Cook fettuccine according to package; drain. Add cooked fettuccine, mozzarella, cream and egg yolks. Stir to blend well. Allow to heat for 15 to 30 minutes. For serving turn to low for up to 30 minutes. Serves 6.

Vegetable Crock Pot

8 potatoes
1 onion, chopped
4 carrots, peeled and sliced
2 stalks celery, sliced
4 chicken bouillon cubes
1 tablespoon parsley flakes
5 cups water
1/3 cup butter or margarine
Ham - cubed to taste
13 ounce can evaporated milk

Peel & cut potatoes into bite-sized pieces. Put all ingredients except evaporated milk in crock pot. Cover and cook 10 to 12 hours. Stir in evaporated milk during last hour. Add flour to thicken, if desired.

Vegetable Soup

2 lb. soup bones or 1 lb. beef short ribs
2 qt. water
1 tsp. salt
1 tsp. celery salt
1 sm. onion, chopped
1 c. carrots, diced
1/2 c. celery, diced
2 c. potatoes, diced

1 lb. cans whole kernel corn, undrained
1 lb. can tomatoes or home canned, cut up
2 turnips, peeled and finely chopped

Place the meat, water, salts, onions, carrots and celery in crock pot. Cover and cook on low for 4-6 hours. Remove bones, chop meat and return to pot. Add potatoes, corn, tomatoes and turnips. Cover and cook on high for 2-3 hours more. Serves 10-12.

Vegetables Italian-Style

1 teaspoon salt
1 medium eggplant cut in 1" cubes
2 to 3 medium zucchini, halved & sliced 1/2"
1 large onion, sliced thinly
12 ounces fresh mushrooms, sliced
1 tablespoon olive oil
4 plum tomatoes, sliced 1/4" thick
1 1/2 cups mozzarella cheese, shredded
2 cups tomato sauce
1 teaspoon oregano
Salt and pepper, to taste

Toss eggplant and zucchini with the 1 teaspoon of salt. Place in a large colander over a bowl to drain for about 1 hour. Drain and squeeze excess moisture out. In a large skillet over medium heat, sauté onion, eggplant, zucchini, and mushrooms until slightly tender. In the crock pot, layer 1/3 of the vegetables (including sliced tomatoes), 1/3 of the tomato sauce. And 1/3 of the cheese. Sprinkle with oregano, salt and pepper. Repeat layering 2 more times. Cover and cook on low 6 to 8 hours. Serve over rice, pasta, or other grain. Serves 6.

Velveeta Salsa Dip

1 pound Velveeta cheese spread, cubed (can use light
1 package picante sauce or salsa
2 tablespoons cilantro (optional)

Place brick of Velveeta and jar of picante sauce in a crock pot or crock pot, and turn on high stirring occasionally until melted and blended. Stir in cilantro when melted. Serve with tortilla chips.

Venison Roast

1 sm. to med. venison roast
1 can cream of mushroom soup
1 pkg Lipton onion soup mix
1 lg. onion, sliced
Soy sauce
Worcestershire sauce
Garlic salt
Season all

Cut venison into serving size piece while meat is raw. Place cleaned and washed meat in crock pot, sprinkle very generously with Worcestershire sauce, soy sauce, season all and garlic salt. Add mushroom soup and onion soup mix. Stir together and place onion rings on top. Cover and cook on low for 6 to 8 hours. the beauty of this recipe is that it only takes a few minutes to prepare early in the morning and can cook all day while you are away to be ready to eat which you get home. Though no water is added, there will be lots of gravy that can be served over rice or potatoes.

Venison Stew

3 carrots
5 potatoes
2 lb. meat, in 1 1/2 inch cubes
1 c. water
1 tsp. Worcestershire sauce
1 clove garlic
1 bay leaf
1 stalk celery
3 onions, quartered
1/2 tsp. pepper
Salt to taste
1 tsp. paprika

Put all ingredients into crock pot. Stir to blend spices. Cook on low for 10 to 12 hours or on high for 5 to 6 hours.

Waldorf Astoria Stew

2 lbs. beef - sirloin, cut up (raw)
2 c. potatoes cut in lg. pieces
2 c. carrots cut in lg. pieces
2 c. celery cut in lg. pieces
1 bag frozen onions (small)
1 slice white bread, cut up
1 (16 oz.) can whole tomatoes (and juice)

2 tbsp. dry minced onion
3 tbsp. quick cooking tapioca
1 tbsp. sugar
1 cans tomato soup
Salt to taste
Pepper to taste

Place all in large crock pot. Cover and cook at low setting for 5 hours. Do not stir. Makes 6 to 8 servings. Add additional vegetables; whatever your family likes. 6 to 8 servings.

White Chili With Chicken

1 lb. dry white northern beans
5 1/4 c. chicken broth
2 cloves garlic, minced
1 lg. white onion, chopped
1 tbsp. ground white pepper
1 tsp. salt
1 tbsp. dried oregano
1 tbsp. ground cumin
1/2 tsp. ground cloves
1 (7 oz.) can diced green chilies
5 c. diced cooked chicken breast
1 3/4 c. chicken broth
1 tbsp. diced jalapeno pepper

Flour tortillas
Condiments: shredded Monterey jack cheese sliced black olives chunky salsa sour cream diced avocados

Soak beans in water to cover for 24 hours then drain. In crock pot or large kettle, combine beans, 5 1/4 cup chicken broth, garlic, onion, white pepper, salt, oregano, cumin, cloves. Simmer covered for at least 5 hours until beans are tender. Stir occasionally. Stir in green chilies, chicken and 1 3/4 chicken broth. For hotter taste, add jalapeno. Cover and simmer for 1 hour. Serve with flour tortillas and condiments.

Wild Rice Casserole

1 1/2 c. uncooked long-grained rice
1/2 c. uncooked wild rice
1 envelope dry onion soup mix
1 tbsp. snipped parsley (optional)

4 c. water
1 bunch green onions, chopped
8 oz. fresh or canned mushrooms, sliced
1/4 c. butter or margarine, melted

Combine all ingredients. Pour into lightly greased crock pot. Cover, cook on high 2 1/2 hours, stirring occasionally.

Wings In Sweet And Sour Sauce

16 chicken wings
4 tablespoons wine or balsamic vinegar
1 cup apricot preserves
2 tablespoons peanut butter (optional)
1 cup ketchup
4 tablespoons horseradish
1 cup sweet onion, finely chopped
1 teaspoon hot sauce (optional)
Pat the chicken wings dry and place then in the crock pot. In a bowl, mix together remaining ingredients. Taste-check for a good balance of sweet and sour. Pour the sauce over the wings. Cover the crock pot and cook on low until the chicken is tender, about 4 hours.

Yummy Chicken Wings

12-18 chicken wings
1/3 c soy sauce
1 tsp. ginger
2 garlic cloves minced
2 green onions minced
1 tbs honey
2 tsp. oil

Combine ingredients in your crock pot. Cook on low for 6-8 hours serves 2-4 people depending on appetizer or main dish

Zucchini Bread

2 eggs
2/3 c. vegetable oil
1 1/4 cup sugar
1 1/3 c. zucchini, peeled and grated
2 tsp. vanilla
2 c. flour

1/4 tsp. salt
1/2 tsp. baking powder
1 tsp. cinnamon
1/2 tsp. nutmeg
1/2 to 1 c. chopped nuts

With mixer, beat eggs until light and foamy. Add oil, sugar, grated zucchini and vanilla. Mix well. Stir dry ingredients with nuts. Add to zucchini mixture. Mix well. Pour into greased and floured 2 pound coffee can or 2 quart mold. Place in crock pot. Cover top with 8 paper towels. Cover and bake on high 3 to 4 hours. Do not check or remove cover until last hour of baking. Let stand 5 minutes before unmolding.

Zucchini Casserole

1 red onion, sliced
1 green pepper cut in thin strips
4 med. zucchini, sliced & unpeeled
1 (16 oz.) can diced tomatoes, undrained
1 tsp. salt
1/2 tsp. pepper
1/2 tsp. basil
1 tbsp. oleo
1/4 c. grated parmesan cheese

Combine all ingredients, except oleo and cheese, in a crock pot. Set temperature on low and heat for 3 hours. Dot casserole with oleo and sprinkle with cheese. Cook 1 1/2 hours more on low setting. Makes 6 servings.

9 781456 317911